BLESSED POSSIBILITIES

Gary M. Douglas

IN CONVERSATION WITH
DR. DAIN HEER AND PARTICIPANTS
AT AN ACCESS CONSCIOUSNESS
SEVEN-DAY EVENT

Published by
Access Consciousness Publishing, LLC
www.accessconsciousnesspublishing.com

Printed in the United States of America

Ease, Joy and Glory

This book is based on conversations between Access Consciousness founder Gary Douglas and the participants at an Access Consciousness seven-day event that took place at a wonderful resort in New Zealand.

Access Consciousness seven-day events are invitation-only, free form classes that are held by Gary three times a year in beautiful locations around the world. To be invited, you must have attended at least one Access Consciousness Choice of Possibilities class in person.

There are no rules, form, or structure to these classes. Gary discusses and creates processes for any subject participants ask about. Everything is included. No question is refused. No topic is banned. It is a class in which you get to explore you and the infinite possibilities for expansion in intimate detail and with brutal honesty. There is no other class or event like this offered anywhere in the world. It is a unique and life-changing experience.

(Participants' names have been replaced with initials unrelated to their actual names.)

Foreword

In the conversations that follow, there may be some words and concepts you have never encountered before. We have tried to define many of them in a glossary at the end of the book.

You will also find the clearing statement we use in Access Consciousness. It's short-speak that addresses the energies that are creating the limitations and contractions in your life. When you first read it, it may twist your head around a little bit. That's our intention. It's designed to get your mind out of the picture so you can get to the energy of a situation.

Basically, with the clearing statement, we're addressing the energy of the limitations and barriers that keep us from moving forward and expanding into all of the spaces that we would like to go.

The Access Consciousness clearing statement is: "Right and Wrong, Good and Bad, POD and POC, All 9, Shorts, Boys and Beyonds®." There is a brief explanation of what the words mean at the end of the book.

You can choose to use the clearing statement or not; I don't have a point of view about that, but I do want to invite you to try it and see what happens.

Table of Contents

What is Phenomenance?

Gary:

Welcome, everyone. I love New Zealand because it has great water—and more water. It's got no snakes, which makes me happy, and we have this wonderful place to spend the next seven days. I don't know whether you have noticed, but the sense of peace that exists here is usually what we get at the *end* of a seven-day event, not at the beginning. Somehow when we returned here, the Earth went right back to where we were the last time we came. It is resonating for us the way we need it to. This is what you want to look at here. This is what you want to feel. This is what you want to take home with you to implement in the rest of the world … because you can.

One day Dain and I were talking about what we could do to change the situation in Fukushima, where some sources say they are releasing ten times more radiation into the ocean than is being reported. We were looking at how we could create something greater and we invited people all over the planet to contribute energy to Fukushima simultaneously. At the time, Dain was in Melbourne and I was in Los Angeles. I thought I had the times right—but I got them mixed up, so we weren't working together simultaneously. Dain got furious with me. He was so pissed he wanted to kill me.

Dain:

No, I wanted to kill Gary *after* I left Access. I wasn't just angry. It was "I'm angry and I'm done! Bye bye." I can't remember ever being that angry. I was also really miserable, and after a while, I called Gary and said, "I need your help, please, because this sucks." Gary asked, "What did I do wrong?"

I looked at it and said, "Wow, you didn't do anything wrong. I think this is a place I need to get past something I haven't been able to get past before."

Gary asked, "What are you not being? What are you not doing?" and we looked at it. He asked, "Is it creation?" and then he said, "Wait a minute! It's bigger than that. You're not being a phenomenon. You're not willing to be the phenomenon you are." When he said that, I heard "phenomenance."

Gary:

And when Dain said, "phenomenance," I said, "Yes, that's it!" Instead of being the phenomenance, the phenomena on planet Earth, we keep trying to create the way other people do. For example, I once noticed that I was saying, "I need to have a hundred million dollars to do all the things I want to do. Where's my gold mine? Where's my diamond mine? Where's my oil well?" Then I said, "Wait! Those are all this reality's solutions for the creation of money. What if there's a different possibility for the creation of money?" And there is! It's *phenomenance*. I'm so grateful that Dain got mad at me. If he hadn't, we wouldn't have found this, and without this, the possibilities in the world would have been minor and not totally blessed.

Phenomenance is the ability to create that which is so far beyond this reality that it is considered a phenomenon, a phenomenal thing, something that doesn't match anybody else's reality.

You have to be willing to be a phenomenon. You have to be willing to be phenomenal, which means you will say and do things without knowing where they come from—and they will work. I'm not talking about having an extraordinary life, which is a life that has all the ordinary stuff plus a little bit extra. What I'm shooting for is phenomenal. It's beyond this reality. That's what we're going to talk about for the next seven days: *phenomenance.*

Phenomenance is where you move beyond the ordinary and the extraordinary (the extra of the ordinary) into that which does not create or compute in this reality. You become a creator when you are being the phenomenance. You become the phenomenance of a different possibility.

Have you ever created anything beyond other people's reality—but you keep acting like you are ordinary? Are you really good at doing ordinary?

If you truly choose phenomenance, you will lose everything that is considered normal in this reality. Your normalcy will go away and all you will have left is extreme potency. That is the choice you have.

To be phenomenance and to function as phenomenance, you must move outside of time. You must move outside of dimensions and outside of reality. You create your life outside of those things, because that's where you are—on the creative edge of blessed possibilities at all times.

The most phenomenal things happen when you are willing to step into phenomenance. All kinds of things can show up in your life. You can do things you never thought were possible. Things begin to talk to you and tell you how to create. When you function from possibilities and you ask: "What's really possible here?" a whole new world is going to open up for you. The whole universe wants to contribute to you. The world wants to contribute to you. The world wants to give you everything you desire—but you don't ask.

What have you made so vital about never possessing phenomenance that keeps you from being? Everything that is times a godzillion, will you destroy and uncreate it all? Right and Wrong, Good and Bad, POD and POC, All 9, Shorts, Boys, and Beyonds.

PN:

Why do you say "possessing phenomenance"?

Gary:

Possessing phenomenance is demanding that you will have total control and ownership over whatever it is—and you are not going to let anything show up except that. That's possession.

What have you made so vital about never possessing phenomenance that keeps you from being? Everything that is times a godzillion, will you destroy and uncreate it all? Right and Wrong, Good and Bad, POD and POC, All 9, Shorts, Boys, and Beyonds.

*Phenomenance is the ability to create that which
is so far beyond this reality that it is considered a
phenomenon, a phenomenal thing, or something that is a
phenomenon that doesn't match anybody else's reality.*

BEING YOU

None of you have a bloody clue what *being* is. You think *being* means "I don't have to do anything." No, truly *being* means you get to do everything you have never done. If you are truly being, you get to choose anything and everything.

What have you made so vital about never possessing phenomenance that keeps you from being? If you were truly being you, would you do things that destroy your life or make your life harder and more difficult? No. So you keep choosing that for what reason? Cuckoo. Cuckoo. Cuckoo.

Everything that is times a godzillion, will you destroy and uncreate it all? Right and Wrong, Good and Bad, POD and POC, All 9, Shorts, Boys, and Beyonds.

*The whole universe wants to contribute to you.
The world wants to contribute to you.
The world wants to give you everything you desire
—but you don't ask.*

Blessed Possibilities

Gary:

The blessed choice of possibility is the way the universe can contribute to you and create something you never knew was possible. You, as an infinite being, have infinite choice, infinite question, infinite possibilities, and infinite contribution, but you are rejecting the gift of possibility. If somebody suggests something that doesn't fit the reality you have, you reject it. If something doesn't fit the way you want it said, it's not going to be part of your reality. You say, "It's got to be said the way I want to hear it." Your need to hear things the way you want to hear them is in the way of the blessed possibilities that are available to you. You aren't willing to hear things the way they come to you. You reject possibilities when you say, "Well, that wasn't what I thought it was."

When a possibility shows up for me, I say:
- Wow, that showed up different than I thought it would!
- What else is possible?
- What else can I choose beyond this?
- And what else can I choose because of this?

Blessed possibilities are about recognizing the blessing that choice is and the gift you are when you are in question. When you are in question and you choose something, you create multiple possibilities.

ND:

I'm pretty cool with things looking different than I think they will. Where am I rejecting possibilities?

Gary:

"Pretty cool with" means "I kind of receive things looking different" or "I reject them slightly." Instead, you've got to ask: "What possibility do I have here that I have never considered?" Be in the question more.

You like to come to conclusions and answers. You like to know that you are going to get it right. You like to know that something is going to work the way you want it to work. You have a tendency to decide what it is going to be instead of being in the question "What is the possibility here?"

This is the way most of you are screwing up your lives. You're looking for a conclusion rather than asking a question that would create a possibility you have never chosen or considered. The blessing of possibilities is the possibility of something you have never even considered.

Have you lived your life by your reality or somebody else's? When you live your life by somebody else's reality, nothing that does not match their reality can even come into your awareness, so you don't have total choice. You've got to get to the place where you are willing to have total choice and total possibility—with no point of view about how it shows up or what it looks like when it shows up. And you have to be willing not to be right ever again.

The blessing of possibilities is the possibility
of something you have never even considered.

POSSIBILITY VS. POTENTIAL

The greatest gift you have is the blessing of possibility. Blessed possibilities are never based on anything. They are about opening to the choice of new possibility and to the question of what *can* get created instead of the conclusion of what *should* be created. *Potential* is what you *think* is going to happen or what can happen based on something else happening.

KS:

Is potential always a conclusion?

Gary:

Yes, potential is always a conclusion. If you say, "This investment has great potential," you have already concluded what the potential is. You have decided it's great—but you have no idea what might be possible if you choose something even greater. Other things could occur that you haven't even considered.

Say you invest in a stock. You think it is a gold mine, and it turns out that they sold the gold mine and have something else going on that will completely change the way cars are produced. The *possibility* of the technological aspect in car production is far greater than the *potential* of the gold mine.

When you tap into the energy of *possibility*, there is always something greater than *potential* can give you.

PR:

You have talked about the energetics of limitation and how it is subtly impelled at us and we make choices from that. What is the way to undo that?

Gary:

You undo the energetics of limitation by looking at the possibilities—not the potentials. Were you ever told that you were not living up to your potential? I was told that 8,000 times, and I would get so pissed. "What the hell does that mean?" I could never figure out what that meant! I don't think that you are not living up to your potential. I think that *you are not choosing your possibilities.* I live my life from:

+ What possibility could I choose here that would create something greater than I have ever been able to create before?
+ What is possible that I have never even considered?
+ What is possible that is so far beyond this reality that nobody else will be able to tap into it?

CHOOSING FOR THE POSSIBILITY

PR:

So you go for seeing the possibility?

Gary:

It is not *seeing* the possibility. It is *choosing* for the possibility, even though you have no idea what it looks like. The possibilities are based on the *energy* you can perceive, not on the vision you can receive. When you *look for* what the possibility is going to be, you are looking for the potential of it, not the possibility of it. You keep trying to see what the vision is going to *look* like. You have spent your entire life trying to strain your vision into something that would create. The possibility is not a straining of vision. It's *an awareness* throughout your entire body.

LM:

What would it take for me to be aware of the invisible possibilities?

Gary:

Are they actually invisible? Or are they just not chosen? You think they are invisible because you will not perceive them as possibilities. You are always willing to look at the potential, aren't you?

LM:

Yeah.

Gary:

You've got to go beyond looking at the potential and ask: "What are the possibilities that I have never even considered?"

> *The possibility is not a straining of vision.*
> *It's an awareness throughout your entire body.*

The Phenomenance of Money

PR:

You and Dain talk about how money is a tool for creating something greater. Can you talk about that in terms of phenomenance?

Gary:

The phenomenance of money is the recognition that money can be used to create a different reality—without having the sense that anyone else needs to understand, see, or follow what you are doing.

DT:

At first I thought the phenomenance of money meant an amount of money that you have, but it's not that. It is the possibility that the money can create and generate.

Gary:

Yes, it's the possibility of what money can create and generate. Once when I was in L.A., I went out to lunch. Somebody handed me $4,000. I put it in my pocket and didn't realize until after we left that the money had fallen out on the couch where we were sitting. I called the restaurant and they said, "Yes, we found some money on the couch. How much was it? We want to make sure it's the same amount." ND went to pick it up. I said, "Give $400 to the woman who found the money. It was ten percent of the amount as a thank you. The woman was totally blown away when ND gave it to her.

RR:

I would also do that, but I don't get that it's phenomenal.

Gary:

Many years ago, I found $2,000 that someone had lost, and the guy gave me $20 for returning it to him. I said, "You know what? That's not acknowledging the fact that someone was honest. That's not gifting something that makes it worthwhile for someone to choose to be that honest." Most people expect you to return their stuff because it is due them or because it is theirs, or because of some other thing. I was willing to give the woman $400.

The phenomenance of money is the recognition of how money can change things. Most people use money to create a result for themselves. They do a business in order to make profit. They don't use money as a way of creating a different reality.

The phenomenance of money is about the recognition that money can be used to create a different reality.

MONEY IS A TOOL FOR CREATING SOMETHING GREATER

If you have a point of view about money like "My partner isn't making enough money. He needs to make more money," is that working with the phenomenance? Or is that working with this reality? That's this reality! And what question is "He is not making enough money"? It's not a question! A question would be "How can I assist him in creating way more money than he ever thought was possible?" or "How can I out-create him so much that he gets inspired to create money?" If you out-create people, they become inspired. Don't try to make people do things. Out-create what they're doing and they'll say, "I've got to have more."

"He's not doing enough," "She's not doing enough," "They're not doing enough," "They're not contributing enough," "They're not, they're not, they're not...." That's not phenomenance. That's the insanity of this reality. Have you noticed that this reality is frigging insane? If you are a phenomenance, you can go beyond this reality with great ease. That's where I am looking to take you. That's my target. If you make it, good, and if you don't, oh well, you can go and work at McDonald's.

When my kids were little and didn't want to go to school, I would say, "It's okay. You don't have to go to school. You can always get a job at McDonald's." They would say, "I would never work at McDonald's!" Telling them that they could work at McDonald's always inspired them to go back to school or do whatever they needed to do to make things work.

What have you made so vital about never possessing the phenomenance of money that keeps you in pathetic and poor and "Oh my God, I wish I had some"? Everything that is times a godzillion, can you destroy and uncreate it all? Right and Wrong, Good and Bad, POD and POC, All 9, Shorts, Boys, and Beyonds.

What if it was never about "I used to have money" or "I will have money in the future"? What if it's "What can I do right now that's going to create all the money I would like to have?" That is where I function from. Am I ever satisfied with the amount of money I get? Never. Why? Because there is always room for more. My caboose has room for lots of money.

You will have an extraordinary life but you will not have a phenomenal one because you're not going to create something that is beyond what anybody else can see.

What have you made so vital about never possessing the phenomenance of money that keeps you from creating beyond this reality? Everything that is times a godzillion, can you destroy and uncreate it all? Right and Wrong, Good and Bad, POD and POC, All 9, Shorts, Boys, and Beyonds.

PR:

I usually don't have challenges with money, but building up to this class my money flows suddenly got really weird. What was that?

Gary:

Other people affect your money flows by their unwillingness to change. They affect your money flows in the sense that they will put the brakes on so hard that it's like being in a traffic jam. If you are in L.A. or Houston or San Francisco and you are going at the speed of light and someone in front of you slams on their brakes for no apparent reason, you have no choice but to slam on your brakes too, if you don't want to run right over the top of them.

PR:

So if you have somebody like that in your life, what do you do?

Gary:

Run them over. Create beyond them. Ask: "Okay, how do I out-create this person's need to hold things in place?" Out-creating somebody's need to hold things in place is the gift you are. It's the phenomenance you are when you are being you. People cannot hold their braking systems in place if you are willing to be everything that you are, because you will just drive right over the top of them. You won't even notice. You'll just keep on moving.

Out-creating somebody's need to hold things
in place is the gift you are.
It's the phenomenance you are when you are being you.

REJECTING MONEY

MP:

I created quite a lot of money in the last week, but it wasn't from my Access business. When I got the money, it was "Oh yeah, that's cool." But if I had made that sort of money with my Access business, I would have been blown away and so happy.

Gary:

Why weren't you happy with the fact that you were able to create that kind of money? Personally I don't care where it comes from as long as I get to create it.

MP:

I get that it's insane.

Gary:

You tend to reject money.

PN:

Is there a process where we can un-reject it?

Gary:

What have I made so vital about rejecting money that absolutely avoids creating it?

Everything that is times a godzillion, will you destroy and uncreate it all? Right and Wrong, Good and Bad, POD and POC, All 9, Shorts, Boys, and Beyonds.

Do you know why you reject money? You are trying to prove you don't need money. It's superiority. Many of you do this. You reject money then you work really hard to get it so you can prove you are able to get it when you want it. I'm glad some of you see how insane that is. You keep wondering why I say, "Cuckoo. Cuckoo. Cuckoo." It's because you are cuckooheads.

Everything that is times a godzillion, will you destroy and uncreate it all? Right and Wrong, Good and Bad, POD and POC, All 9, Shorts, Boys, and Beyonds.

Aren't we miraculous? It's a miracle that you have managed to do any of the things you have done while working so hard against you to make sure you can prove to you that you are powerful enough to get what you want without having everything that you truly desire instantaneously. You want a hard life—but the only thing that is supposed to be hard is your penis.

MP:

Is there something underneath this that is holding it in place? I have been aware of this for ages.

Gary:

It's the fact that you don't care.

MP:

That I don't care about money? Or that I just don't care?

Gary:

That you don't care about money *and* you just don't care.

MP:

Is that a good thing or a bad thing? Or is it just that I don't care?

Gary:

Well, it's a choice. The question is: What does your choice create?

MP:

Well, it's not creating ease with my body.

Gary:

Oh yeah, that! And why does one have money? Because the body needs money. You, the infinite being, don't. Duh!

What have you made so vital about rejecting and refusing money that absolutely avoids creating it? Everything that is times a godzillion, will you destroy and uncreate it all? Right and Wrong, Good and Bad, POD and POC, All 9, Shorts, Boys, and Beyonds.

"What does your choice create?"

REFUSING MONEY

VT:

I perceive that people refuse money because they want to be liked. If you are filthy, stinking rich, there is the perception that people hate you. Is it that people aren't willing to receive money—or is it that they aren't willing to be not liked?

Gary:

They are not willing to be liked for their money.

VT:

Whatever JT and I have and whatever we create, I can't say that we have had more people like us or more people dislike us. But in the end, who cares?

Gary:

That's my point of view. "Who cares?"

A lot of people create "no money" in order to create necessity. That's their motivating factor. Lack of money motivates them to do things. What if lack of money wasn't a motivating factor? What if having money was a creative factor for a greater possibility?

JT:

Yes, because when you have money, you have the ability to create more money.

Gary:

And it is not just money you get to create. You get to create a change in the world. And it's not about the amount of money that you have. It is about the moment when you know that the thing you've done will change something. That's why I gave $400 to the lady who returned the money I left behind. That blew her mind. She didn't expect that.

It's not about the amount of money you have.
It is about the moment when you know that the
thing you've done will change something.

WHAT DO YOU WANT TO CREATE IN THE WORLD?

ND:

So what's it going to take for us to choose to have money for consciousness?

Gary:

Well, you have to see what it is you want to create in the world. Could I create more of what I really want to have in the world if I had more money? Yeah. You've got to come from that point of view. I asked, "How much more money would I have to have to create all the things I want to create on the planet?" That's when I realized "Okay, I need $100 million."

I'd like to have $100 million because I could finish El Lugar ("The Place") in a heartbeat. El Lugar is a not-for-profit resort and education center we are starting to develop in Costa Rica, a place where people come to learn to live with the elegance of the Earth and not abuse it. I would have it done in less than two years. Everybody says, "Oh, you can't possibly do that in less than four years." Watch me! I would create a teachers' college. Actually I would go out and buy a teachers' college and teach everybody how to teach by Access standards. Then they would go out in the world and get jobs in private schools that would become famous for their great education instead of their great babysitting. All of it would contribute to greater possibilities. What else could I create? I would probably create a hospital dedicated to doing something different. A lady called me and said she wants to introduce Access to people who are coming back from Iran and Iraq with post-traumatic stress disorder. They are committing suicide to the point that it is crippling her organization.

I said, "Yes, use it."

She asked, "What do I owe you?"

I said, "Nothing, just acknowledge that you got it from Access. I don't care about the rest of it."

For me, it's what else can we create in the world that we haven't yet created?

- If you didn't have money as an issue, where could you put yourself?
- Where could you put your time?
- Where could you put your energy?
- Where could you put the elements of the things you have learned, to create something greater?
- What do you know that other people don't know that if you gave them that education would create a different source in the world?

USING MONEY TO CREATE BEYOND THIS REALITY

JW:

How do I learn to have the phenomenance of creating money?

Gary:

By running this process:

What have you made so vital about never possessing the phenomenance of money do you use to keep you from creating beyond this reality? Everything that is times a godzillion, will you destroy and uncreate it all? Right and Wrong, Good and Bad, POD and POC, All 9, Shorts, Boys, and Beyonds.

Then you ask a question: "What could I practice today that would create more money than I have ever had before?" You also need to ask: "What can I practice?" You are going to have to practice because you are crap at creating money. You just want it to magically show up in your bank account.

JW:

Yes, I will practice. Last year in a class you had someone ask me, "What do you hate about having money?" I did that question at home with my husband, and we got between twenty and forty different points of view. It was amazing.

Gary:

Most of you don't realize that you have a godzillion points of view about money.

JW:

I was totally shocked. I had always thought I was poor. Through you, I learned that I have never been poor. That is new for me, and now I am willing to learn the phenomenance of creating money.

Gary:

Good, you will then.

"NEVER ENOUGH MONEY BUT ALWAYS TOO MUCH TO SPEND"

VT:

I really like the process you shared with us a while ago. It is a really simple ONE:

"Never enough money but always too much to spend." I have been running that one ever since you gave it to us.

Gary:

It is designed to take away your thought process because it does not compute. It's not a logical point of view. And when it is not a logical point of view, you can't put it into the computational world that people define as valuable. It has been working for you, hasn't it? Money is growing.

VT:

Yes, I don't think about it. I just do it.

ND:

We're all such phenomenal creators. How come we don't all have millions in the bank?

Gary:

Because you have never cared about it. Having millions or billions of dollars has never been your criterion for existence or creation. But what if you could have that *and* everything else? It's not an either/or. Money is one of the things you can add to your life.

WHAT IF HAVING MONEY WAS A CREATIVE FACTOR FOR A GREATER POSSIBILITY?

TS:

When you mentioned creating a different kind of hospital, I thought about psychiatric hospitals. It is so easy to make it about the money and say, "I don't have the money to do that." But that's not it. It's about being the source for the creation of that, isn't it?

Gary:

Yes, that's the reason you used to get confused when you'd ask, "What do I need to do?" and I'd say "BE." When you are willing to *be*, you can ask: "Okay, what would it take to create the money, because I'd like this to go further. I'd like this to go faster, I'd like this to be bigger. I'd like something greater here. What's it going to take to create that?"

TS:

When I see a piece of jewelry I like, I say, "I'm having this, thank you very much." And the money shows up. It could be that easy with everything else.

Gary:

It could be that easy with everything. For VT, money is easy. He doesn't think it's hard. He says, "Oh, money is easy. You just do blah, blah, blah." And people go "Huh?" I talked to him once for twenty minutes and I said, "I want to have what he is having. I want that kind of ease with money, where I just say, "Okay fine, I'll do that."

TS:

Don't you have that?

Gary:

Pretty much, but I would like to have it at a bigger level than I currently have. I want way more.

TS:

What you just said about having it at a bigger level is great.

Gary:

If you are going to create you as the source for creating a different world, you've got to be willing to function at a bigger level than anybody else around you.

That is a place where you are willing to be the phenomenance of change in the world. You are willing to be the phenomenance of that changes the world. I'd like you to get to the place where you ask: "Wow, what could I do that would change the world?" Not "What could I do to make more money?" Not "What could I do to have more cars or more houses?" Not "What could I do to not make people angry?" Not "What could I do to make sure that we make it through the next day?"

What would it be like if you were actually willing to be the gift of change you truly are? What have you made so vital about never being the source of change on planet Earth that keeps you from the phenomenance of being? Everything that is times a godzillion, will you destroy

and uncreate it all? Right and Wrong, Good and Bad, POD and POC, All 9, Shorts, Boys, and Beyonds.

If you are going to create you as the source for creating a different world, you've got to be willing to function at a bigger level than anybody else around you.

The Phenomenance of Generosity of Spirit

Gary:

Dain and I once went to a lodge where people pay $2,000 a night for accommodation. The place was gorgeous, and the people had come for golf, tennis, and hot tubbing. The guests there were not interested in creating anything with their money. They were only interested in showing that they could afford to stay there. Unfortunately, there were a lot of mean people there and very few happy people. And in a place that beautiful, you should be happy and not mean. If you are going to spend that kind of money, at least be happy about the fact that you spent it!

One night at dinner, Dain and I ordered the last bottle of a particular kind of wine. Some other people in the dining room ordered it as well, and the waiter said, "I'm sorry, I just sold my last bottle to those two gentlemen over there."

I said, "We'll split it with you." We gave them half a bottle of wine.

They said, "We'll split the bill."

I said, "No, we're giving it to you. It's a gift."

They didn't say, "Thank you, that's so kind." They said, "Oh, then we'll give you a half bottle of wine too." That was the energy of not receiving. They only had an interest in proving they didn't need what they had been given so they wouldn't have to say, "Thank you." They were showing us that they were rich, not that they were wealthy. Wealth has generosity of spirit. Richness does not. Generosity of spirit is a phenomenance, and you either have it or you don't. It's not something you can create.

PR:

So you are either born with it or you're not?

Gary:

Yes, you either come in with it or you don't. In sharing our wine with those people in the restaurant, I wasn't trying to get anything from them. I was sharing what I had. They had no interest in sharing or receiving our gift.

You have to know what people will receive and not assume they are capable of receiving anything. We keep trying to do things for people or give things to people that they can't receive and have no interest in. They have no interest in what we are offering. They don't have an interest in what we want to give them. They have no interest in anything except proving what they have decided they have to prove in life.

WHATEVER YOU HAVE IS A GIFT

CL:

Did you say generosity of spirit can't be learned or cultivated? I'm asking because I would say that has changed a lot for me over the years I have been in Access.

Gary:

Yes, your generosity of spirit has increased, but you had it in the beginning. You had generosity of spirit when you were a little girl and your mom gave you some paper as a Christmas present, and you said, "Mommy, it's paper! Oh my goodness! I got paper!" You thought life was wondrous. Generosity of spirit is the sense that whatever you get or whatever you have is a gift to you, and that the universe is doing its best for you.

It is not what you give. It's about the gift that life is and the way you perceive it. It is the way you receive the world and the way the world receives you. The story about you getting paper cracked me up because it was so cute. Here's a little person who has nothing. She gets paper for Christmas and considers it a great gift.

Generosity of spirit is the sense that whatever you get or whatever you have is a gift to you, and that the universe is doing its best for you.

PAYING FOR EVERYTHING

ND:

I do generosity of spirit but I do this other weird thing too. I don't want money to be a factor for people, so I automatically want to cover the bill for their food, drinks, or hotel room. It's like an auto-response system.

Gary:

That's trying to prove how superior you are.

ND:

Maybe, but it doesn't feel like it is coming from trying to prove something. It's automatic.

Gary:

You've automated it because you don't want to owe anything to anyone. If you pay for everything, then you can dismiss anybody at will.

ND:

Yeah, that's it. What do I do about that?

Gary:

You can look at it and ask, "Do I really want to do that?" I used to pay for everything because I thought that if I paid for everything, I didn't have to receive from anybody. My lovely crew beat the shit out of me a month or so ago and I started letting them contribute. Now we all pay for dinners and stuff instead of just me. It's quite cool.

At first it was obnoxious to have to receive. I hated the fact that I had to receive under those conditions because as long I was doing all the giving, I didn't have to receive much of anything. It was a major change for me, and I have now stopped doing the automatic response of paying for everything. When you pay for everything, the tendency is to never be obligated. You have the sense that when you let others pay for you that you somehow owe them.

I had a couple of very wealthy clients that I took out to dinner all the time. Every time they asked me to go to dinner with them, they would keep their credit cards in their pockets and wait for me to pay. I'd think, "Wow, you guys are really generous." They weren't interested in what they had received from me. They were interested in my paying to make it real to them that they were valuable. My paying made them valuable from their point of view. Is that really what makes someone valuable? No. You've got to get that there's a different possibility available. You just have to choose it.

It is not what you give. It's about the gift that life is and the way you perceive it.
It is the way you receive the world and the way the world receives you.

GLADNESS

DT:

In this reality, do people mix up the meaning of being generous and having generosity of spirit?

Gary:

Yes. Being generous means you pay for everything. Generosity of spirit is gladness for everything.

DT:

Is generosity of spirit similar to the exuberant expression of life and abundance in all things? And if you truly have generosity of spirit when you are being generous, it comes from an exuberant expression of life and abundance?

Gary:

Exactly.

DT:

It's not about paying for people.

Gary:

That's correct; it is not about the money. It is about the *possibilities* you are creating. It's never about the money you are spending or the money the other person is not spending.

CL:

This has been really helpful. I see that I replaced generosity of spirit with generosity. That's why I was confused, because lately I have been way more generous in terms of gifting and paying.

Gary:

Yes, you have been way more generous with money and less generous with you.

CL:

Yeah.

Generosity of spirit is gladness for everything.

THE GLAD GAME

Gary:

How many of you watched *Pollyanna* as a kid? Did you play the Glad Game? Pollyanna is generosity of spirit. It's never seeing the wrongness of what somebody chooses, always knowing that somebody is choosing something that works for them, and having no point of view about it. It's being willing to show them that they can have more if they are willing to choose something different.

I highly recommend that all of you watch *Pollyanna* again. What are you glad for? What are you happy for? What are you happy for other people having in their life? What if you saw that every prism was another form of rainbow? What if you saw that every element, every ray of sunshine, was a gift and possibility?

Blessed possibility is recognizing the gift that each and every thing is, each and every spirit that comes to you, each and every bird that sits on your window sill. This morning I was getting ready and I went over to the window to see what was happening outside. There was a little bird sitting there. I said, "Hi, you're cute." I moved over to the other side and I saw that there were two more of them. All three of them were sitting with their little feathers fluffed out because they were cold. I said, "Aw, I'm sorry if you're cold. How about I ask the sun to come and warm you up?" And a beam of sunlight opened up on them. That's the kind of thing that can occur when you have generosity of spirit. Knowing that this creature needed a little sun is a different reality.

What are you glad for?

MAKING MONEY THE SOURCE OF YOUR GENEROSITY

ND:

I still don't see the difference between having generosity of spirit, communing with a bird, being kind to someone, and paying for something. To me, it's all the same energy.

Gary:

But how do other people receive it? You're not willing to see what people can receive. You are doing it for *you*, not for *them*. With animals you can see the generosity of spirit because you are not doing it *for* them; you are doing it *with* them. When you pay for things, the tendency is to do it *for* the other person or for you, rather than *with* them. Some of you are trying to make your money the source of your generosity.

AN:

Yeah.

Gary:

Those of you who don't have enough money think that you have no generosity because you can't give people money. Not being able to give money does not mean you lack generosity. Even if you have money and you give it to people, when you are not happy for who those people are, you are not being generous. You don't need to have money to have generosity of spirit, but you can use money to *be* generosity of spirit.

> *Even if you have money and you give it to people,*
> *when you are not happy for who those people are,*
> *you are not being generous.*

THE RECOGNITION OF A GIFT

HB:

I'm not sure I am ready to receive the change this conversation about generosity of spirit is heading toward, but I have to ask this because I struggle with it, especially with NK. You have said several times that it is not about how much you pay, or how much other people pay, or how much they give or do, but I have been stuck…

Gary:

What kind of gift is NK in your life?

HB:

Huge.

Gary:

So if he is a big gift in your life, is that worth something?

HB:

Yes, but this is where this weird energy comes up. I want to say *no*. It's as if I'm fighting to make something wrong.

Gary:

Generosity of spirit is the recognition of the gift. NK is paper in your world. "Oh my goodness, I got paper! Oh my goodness! I got NK, I got NK!"

HB:

Can you help me? It feels like there's a lot more to that.

THE EXCHANGE RATE

Gary:

You have made it vital to have an exchange. Were you taught by anybody in your life that you must always put in an exchange?

HB:

Yeah. On the surface, it's so that I don't get taken advantage of, or used.

Gary:

Stop, stop. You were taught that there had to be an exchange rate for everything.

HB:

I will say *yes* because you are saying so, but I do not know that cognitively. I don't remember times when that was specifically taught to me.

Gary:

When you were a little kid, it was "Give Mommy a kiss because I am so good to you and because I love you."

SM:

Okay, got it. It's not just me. It's done to everybody.

Gary:

Yes. I'm not doing this just for you! There are many people in the room who need to look at this.

How many of you were convinced that you were never enough? Your exchange was never enough for the people that you were with. You are never enough for the people that you are with. That lack of generosity in their world becomes what you think determines your exchange value in a system of reality. Everything that is times a godzillion, will you destroy and uncreate it all? Right and Wrong, Good and Bad, POD and POC, All 9, Shorts, Boys, and Beyonds.

You had somebody forcing down your gullet that you had to have an exchange rate.

HB:

Keep going, yeah, yeah.

Gary:

So you have to look through judgment to determine whether there is an adequate exchange.

HB:

Okay, can you be specific?

Gary:

Hold on, I'm getting there.

You have tried to make an exchange rate that does not actually apply to the people you are functioning with. You keep trying to apply it to everybody and everything around you, and it is not applicable to everybody and everything. Everything that is times a godzillion, will you destroy and uncreate it all? Right and Wrong, Good and Bad, POD and POC, All 9, Shorts, Boys, and Beyonds.

What is your three-year-old nephew's exchange rate with you?

HB:

His exchange rate with *me?*

Gary:

Yes.

HB:

There is no exchange rate.

Gary:

That's right.

HB:

I would give and do anything for him.

Gary:

I know. The exchange rate is his gift of being. His being contributes so much to you that there is no exchange involved. That's why you would do anything for him. What if NK was that contributory to you?

SM:

Well, he is!

Gary:

I know that, but you don't. And he doesn't know.

SM:

That's true. He definitely doesn't know. I'm hearing all of the big notes in this conversation, but you are also hitting a lot of subtle notes.

Gary:

What have you made so vital about possessing exchange that keeps you from enjoying being?

HB:

Exchange is what holds the whole monetary system in place.

Gary:

No, it doesn't. That is what you have been taught and told. You bought a lie. The exchange rate is not the thing that holds monetary reality in place.

HB:

Well, it is an aspect of monetary reality.

Gary:

Not really. If you are willing to pay whatever the rate is, that's not an exchange. It's a choice. You've got to get the *choice* in monetary reality, not the *exchange rate*. This is where you're buying out of the phenomenance of money. You are not seeing that money is merely a choice that can create a different possibility. You are seeing money as what you have to do to get what you want. That is not what it is. What have you made so vital about possessing exchange rates that keeps you from the gift of being?

HB:

It takes all of the joy out of having everything.

Gary:

In NK's family, the exchange rate was "You make yourself nothing, and we will give you money."

HB:

It's not even "We'll give you money." It's "We will give you money… maybe… eventually."

They say to him, "We won't give you any money now because we want some to be left over for you when we die."

Gary:

That's one of the ways people control through the exchange rate of money. "Do this for me now and you will get something in the future."

HB:

It's bizarre with NK's nieces and nephews. When they come to our house, they are out of their minds. They are manic and frantic every time they come over.

Gary:

Whose reality is that?

HB:

Their mom's. They always want us to buy them things. "Will you buy this for me? Will you buy this for me? Will you buy this for me?" I keep buying them things to see when it will tap out, and it never does. I will buy them something and they will literally throw it on the ground and ask, "Will you buy me this other thing?"

Gary:

They have no gladness in their universe.

HB:

That's it. How do you teach somebody that?

Gary:

Make them watch *Pollyanna* twenty-five times. Just say, "Let's watch *Pollyanna* again." You've got to get the Glad Game in place. Ask: "Who is the one person that you are most happy about? Would your life be as good if this person wasn't in it?" You have to function from that.

You are not seeing that money is merely a choice that can create a different possibility.
You are seeing money as what you have to do to get what you want.

GENEROSITY OF SPIRIT CREATES MONEY

MN:

In my family, the only person who had generosity of spirit was my dad. I grew up with his generosity of spirit. You have also had generosity of spirit with me, and so has RD. You guys are the ones I would create the most money with. Is that how it works?

Gary:

Yes. If you have generosity of spirit with people, you will create more money with them.

DT:

I noticed that when you went shopping for your grandson, Xander, the joy in your universe was even greater than the joy when you're buying antiques. Is that the phenomenance of money?

Gary:

Yes, buying things for him is the greatest fun ever.

DT:

When you buy antiques, I can see how it has to do with the phenomenance of money, because it creates different possibilities with your money situation. But when you buy a pair of pants for Xander, does that also create different possibilities? I suppose that when you buy things for him, it is about the joy that you have in your world. Is that the phenomenance of money as well?

Gary:

Yes, the phenomenance of money is where money is not just about spending; it is the joy you get from what you choose. And what you do and where you spend it.

DT:

That is what you do. It's not because of how the other person is going to react. It's the joy you have in your world when you are using your money in that way.

Gary:

Yes, it is *using* money. I don't *spend* my money, I *use* it.

How many of you are spending money instead of using money? Everything you have done to *spend* money instead of *using* money, because the phenomenance of money is "How do I use my money to create something greater?" Everything that is times a godzillion, will you destroy and uncreate it all? Right and Wrong, Good and Bad, POD and POC, All 9, Shorts, Boys, and Beyonds.

CL:

There is so much here for me. I am really grateful for this conversation. I was looking at the energy of when I bought my new car four years ago. I was so excited and that excitement had people really excited with me.

Gary:

Those are people with generosity of spirit. People are excited with you because they see the gift that your excitement is to you—and to them.

When you see someone getting something great, do you say, "Oh my God! That's so great. Oh my goodness, she got a new car"? Most of us don't do that. We say, "Oh yeah, she got a new car." That's the way it's done here. Generosity of spirit has nothing to do with it.

Happiness at what you receive is a gift few people can receive from you. If you got a million dollars tomorrow, how many people would you be willing to tell about it, knowing that they would be glad for you? Most people would say, "How come *you* got it and *I* didn't?"

It's the phenomenance that somebody gets something, and what a gift it is that the universe cares about them enough to give them what they asked for. It is the kindness of it all.

PR:

You said that generosity of spirit is something we are born with. It's not something that is created. What about kindness?

Gary:

Kindness is something you choose. It is a choice you make. Usually you make that choice based on seeing other people's lack of kindness. You say, "That's horrible. I'm not going to have that. I'm going to have a level of kindness that's greater than this." You can choose your reality from that. Kindness is always a choice, just as meanness is always a choice. It's never just a given. It's a choice in every moment of every day.

Kindness is something you choose. It is a choice you make.

RECEIVING THE JOY

PA:

I feel that I have no generosity of spirit. You've gifted me things…

Gary:

And you received them like crap at the beginning, but after a while you said, "Okay, fine." You gave in.

PA:

Can we look at that? I have never been willing to receive the joy of things.

Gary:

No, you have never been willing to receive something that would bring you joy because you didn't want to take it.

How many of you have never been willing to take because you didn't want to lose? Everything that is times a godzillion, will you destroy and uncreate it all? Right and Wrong, Good and Bad, POD and POC, All 9, Shorts, Boys, and Beyonds.

PA:

Have I confused *taking* with *receiving?*

Gary:

Yeah. How many times in your life were you given a gift where somebody didn't expect something in return? Pretty much never.

PA:

Have I not been willing to take because I didn't want to lose?

Gary:

Yeah.

PA:

I get it but I don't get it. I have that with everything. Cars, houses. I've got a point of view that I won't allow myself to be attached to anything. That has messed up the receiving and the joy of it.

Gary:

Yes, and it is also not being glad for everything you have.

PA:

No, I haven't been.

Gary:

You've got to be glad for everything you have. You have to be grateful for it. And you have to say, "Well okay, if this thing wants to move away, it can move away."

PA:

I don't know how to be glad for everything I have.

Gary:

Yes, I know. Watch *Pollyanna*. You all need to watch *Pollyanna*. You need to see that it is about being glad for what you *have*, not sad for what you *don't have*. The majority of people in the world teach you to be sad for what you don't have, rather than to be glad for what you do have, so none of you are satisfied with what you get. But you are very satisfied to be unhappy with what you don't have. Why is that satisfactory?

You've got to be glad for everything you have.

THE REFUSAL OF RECEIVING

NK:

I have a sense of righteousness about not receiving. Can you help me with that?

Gary:

Isn't that what your family taught you? "You are so much better because you don't have to receive." It is the superiority of the refusal of receiving.

NK:

Then you don't have to be at the effect of anybody or have an obligation.

Gary:

Yes, your family says, "You're not obligated by anybody except us, your parents, because we're going to give you money someday… maybe." When do you get to be glad for you being in the world?

What have you made so vital about never possessing the gratitude and gladness for you being in life that keeps you suffering for all eternity? Everything that is times a godzillion, will you destroy and uncreate it all?

Right and Wrong, Good and Bad, POD and POC, All 9, Shorts, Boys, and Beyonds.

What have you made so vital about never possessing the gladness and the joy of being you that keeps you in always suffering and never having? Everything that is times a godzillion, will you destroy and uncreate it all? Right and Wrong, Good and Bad, POD and POC, All 9, Shorts, Boys, and Beyonds.

HB:

I remember several Christmases where I got so much amazing stuff that it was more than I could receive. I've also watched you teach Dain how to do that for his mom. You show people how to give. And when you give people amazing things, there's an incredible value of self that starts being engendered in those people.

Gary:

If somebody else acknowledges how great you are, you *might* acknowledge how great you are, *might* being the operative word.

HB:

My stomach is in knots around this. There is some weird internal conflict I am having.

Gary:

Why are you having an internal conflict? Once you have an internal conflict, it also becomes an eternal conflict.

Everywhere you have created the internal conflict that creates the eternal conflict of you with you, will you destroy and uncreate all that? Right and Wrong, Good and Bad, POD and POC, All 9, Shorts, Boys, and Beyonds.

HB:

I know that with just the flick of a switch I could be everything I know I can be.

Gary:

Okay, but you can't.

HB:

It's more like I won't.

Gary:

I know. Instead of choosing for you regardless of what anybody else says, you want me to convince you why you should be everything you know you can be. What if you could live without this conflict?

HB:

I'm almost there. But this is deep!

Generosity of spirit is the sense that whatever
you get or whatever you have is a gift to you, and
that the universe is doing its best for you.

Happiness

WHAT IS THE VALUE OF FIGHTING HAPPINESS?

EL:

I've been intensely aware of how much violent resistance there is against happiness in the world. It seems like everybody is being violent or violently miserable every minute. People are so *not* happy.

Gary:

They don't want to be happy.

EL:

A couple of years ago, you gave me the process "What's the value of fighting happiness?" It stopped me in my tracks, and I realized that every single thing I had been upset about was my fighting of happiness. That is still the case, but it is getting easier.

Gary:

What have you made so vital about possessing unhappiness that keeps you from all other choices? Not that this will affect any of the rest of you! Everything that is times a godzillion, will you destroy and uncreate it all? Right and Wrong, Good and Bad, POD and POC, All 9, Shorts, Boys, and Beyonds.

Unhappiness is the way we eliminate choice and life.

HB:

That's exactly what's happening. But it feels powerful or correct.

Gary:

It is powerful. Everybody else has the brakes on, and you put yours on too. It is the same way people control your money. They throw the brakes on and then you throw the brakes on too, to make sure you don't crash into their world.

HB:

But you crash into their world anyway.

Gary:

Or you could have a back-to-the-future car and fly over the top of them. Sometimes when people do unhappiness, I say, "Oh you poor thing. I'm so sad for you." Am I? Hell no! Why not? Because their sadness is a creation. It's not a reality. It's an invention. Are you aware of how much people love being unhappy?

HB:

Yes, myself included.

Gary:

Yes, but is that unhappiness yours? Or are you slamming on the brakes because everybody else has the brakes on? Why don't you just fly right over them? Grow wings? If you are a phenomenance, you have the wings to go beyond. You want to settle with a bunch of sheep instead of being with the geese that can fly away.

HAPPINESS WILL HEAL THE EARTH

HB:

What if we are unhappy because of what other people are doing?

Gary:

There's no *reason* to be unhappy. It's just a choice.

HB:

But there's Fukushima or the fracking of the Earth...

Gary:

Happiness will heal the Earth. Unhappiness will kill it.

HB:

So we should be happy that water sources are being destroyed?

Gary:

The only thing that is going to change the outcome of anything on this planet is the happiness that can go beyond the destruction. If everybody in this room was willing to be happy enough to have ten million dollars, we could buy the majority ownership of all of the companies that are doing that kind of shit—and change it. It goes back to this: You have to be willing to be the phenomenance that changes reality.

HB:

So it's just having no point of view? It's having no point of view about what they are doing to the Earth?

Gary:

Do I have a point of view? Yeah. I think it's kind of crazy. It's like the Pakistanis who detonated a bunch of bombs underground and then they had the worst earthquake they had ever had in their history. And they wondered why. You live in earthquake faults and you are blowing up bombs underground to test them. Are you stupid? Apparently.

FB:

Is there anything that we can contribute to stop the fracking that is going on?

Gary:

People who practice benevolent capitalism would never do fracking. For them, it would not be about the amount of money they could make; it would be about what that's going to contribute to the world and the Earth. Mankind has to wake up, and I think, unfortunately, that fracking will open the door to a level of awareness that people have never been willing to choose, because a lot of fracking is being done in places where there are earthquake faults. There have never been earthquakes in those locations, but the fracking will activate the faults and create disasters. That will create a change in the awareness level people have.

What you can do is go on social media and ask questions like:

- Is this really a good idea?
- Aren't we just opening the Earth to earthquake faults?
- What are we going to create with this kind of choice?

Just ask the questions. If you put out the questions, thousands of others are going to come to conclusion, and the conclusion will be "We shouldn't do this." You've got to be the question and the energy to create a different possibility. You've got to be the phenomenance of you, which creates a different reality.

North Korea is testing bombs underground. People try to stop them. I say, "Don't stop them. Encourage them." Talk about their infrastructure going away. The disaster will create the necessity of change. Unfortunately most people will not change until a disaster creates the need of it. Happiness will create possibilities. Disasters will create necessities. If you resist the destruction, you create the necessities.

You can look at fracking and say, "Well, that's really frigging stupid. There are other ways to do it. There are other ways to create possibilities." But nobody is looking to create possibilities. They are looking to do it by the same monetary reality that has always been. That's the reason you have to get the phenomenance of a different financial reality.

HB:

I have been getting sick a lot recently because I have been thinking about the Earth.

Gary:

Then you are going to get sick because you are going to feel the sickness that the Earth feels and you're going to be tapping into the sickness of the people that have to create it that way.

HB:

So should I look at it and say, "Okay, it's silly."

Gary:

It's just an interesting point of view. What if you asked: "What happiness can I be that can change it all?" You kill the Earth with unhappiness. You create it and generate it with happiness.

LY:

A few years ago when we were touring around New Zealand, we became aware of the incredible root systems of the trees and plants here. I had never felt them anywhere else like that. When we returned this time, I became very sad for a few moments because there has been definite death since I was last here. I asked, "What contribution could I be?" and immediately, it was just joy. It was really easy to just change and be joyful.

> *You kill the Earth with unhappiness. You*
> *create it and generate it with happiness.*

IT IS JUST A CHOICE

Gary:

When I was doing a Level Two and Three Class in Houston, there was a little kid who was crying the entire time. His mother said, "I don't know why he is so unhappy."

I said to my three-year-old grandson, "Xander, will you go over and show that little kid how to be happy?" Xander walked over to the kid. He bent down and put all his energy into the kid's universe, and the kid started to laugh. Xander is a kid who knows how to be happy. Why don't you? Happiness is just a choice.

People ask, "What's required for me to be happy?"

I say, "Choice. You just have to choose it." If you actually got happy, who would you have to stop fighting? Yourself. What would you have to do? Have a good time! Was there ever a time when, as a kid, you just got to be a happy little critter that could run up and down and smile? Then you got taught how to be more adult and take responsibility for your toys and stuff. So now you can't just be happy. You have to think about the consequences of your actions.

Everything that brought up for you, will you destroy and uncreate it all? Right and wrong, Good and Bad, POD and POC, All 9, Shorts, Boys, and Beyonds.

HAPPINESS AND JOY

BK:

Is joy bigger than happiness?

Gary:

No, happiness is actually bigger than joy. Happiness is the *being* and joy is the *doing.*

BK:

I feel like I have had a lot of happiness lately.

Gary:

Happiness always has a sense of peace with it. There is a peace in happiness. There is an exuberance in joy. So if you are having exuberance, you are probably doing joy. If you have a sense of peace, there's just the expansiveness of peace and the possibility that occurs.

BK:

Can happiness be exuberant?

Gary:

If it is peaceful, yes. You can make it whatever you want it to be. I am not trying to make you wrong. I am trying to create greater clarity so you have more choice. You can have it any way you want. If you want to have exuberant, joyful happiness, go for it. If you want to have exuberant happiness but not joy, go for it. If you want to have a different reality than anybody else, go for it. It's about the phenomenance of having your own reality. When you have your own reality, you don't have to buy anybody else's point of view—ever.

Happiness is just a choice.

CHOOSING A DARK PLACE

MP:

There's a dark place I go to...

Gary:

This dark place you "go to," it's something you have created as part of your reality. It's your go-to place.

MP:

Why do I do that?

Gary:

"Why?" is the wrong question. A better question would be "I would choose this bullshit for what reason?" And then: "I am not going to have this as part of my reality." You think that if you can come to the reason and justification for something, you can decide whether or not you want to choose it. But you have already chosen it. So how do you change it? By changing it. By saying, "I'm not going to choose this anymore." That dark space is your dominant go-to space. You have to practice not choosing it.

MP:

I have been doing that this week. I have been stepping out from the comfort zone of that go-to place.

Gary:

You just called that dark place a comfort zone. You just let your guard down enough to actually say what it is for you. It's your comfort zone. That's why you don't want to lose it. That's your reason for holding on to it. For whatever reason, it comforts you to have that dark place to go to. The reason and justification for it are irrelevant.

What is a comfort zone for you? I think for HB, judgment is like a comfort zone.

HB:

I can relate to that being a comfort zone.

MP:

Well, I like dark, small spaces. I could live in a cave.

Gary:

Okay, now we've got why you choose it. That's your reason. You should get yourself a large suitcase to sleep in. Or a coffin. Why don't you get a coffin and sleep in that? Or maybe you could just say, "I'm not going to choose this anymore."

"I'm not going to choose this anymore."

YOU HAVE TO PRACTICE BEING HAPPY

GH:

This morning it was so hard to get out of bed. I just wanted to stay there and then I said, "No, just get out of bed." So I got up. I kept asking, "Why is the world so fucked up? Why do we do that? What's the point?" I keep asking, "Why? Why? Why?"

Gary:

I want you to change your question to "Why not? Why not? Why not?" Instead of asking, "Why should I do it?" ask, "Why not do it?" "Why not?" is positive when you ask it.

GH:

It's like I have lost my energy pack. You know the button to press so you can be happy? It fell off. I can't find it anymore. I don't know where it went. That's the best way I can describe it.

Gary:

What have you made so vital about doubt that keeps you from being?

GH:

What do you mean? What have I made so vital about doubt? What have I made so important about doubt?

Gary:

Yeah.

What have you made so vital about doubt that keeps you from creating your life? Everything that is times a godzillion, will you destroy and uncreate it all? Right and Wrong, Good and Bad, POD and POC, All 9, Shorts, Boys, and Beyonds.

GH:

Yeah, but what's the point?

Gary:

To have fun.

GH:

Yeah, I know. I have heard that so many times.

Gary:

That was such a resistance and reaction to "The purpose of life is to have fun."

GH:

I know. People say, "Let's try that" and I say, "But why?"

Gary:

But. "I would do it *but…*" "I would have this *but…*" "I discovered this *but…*" "I want to be happy *but…*" You guys have the "But Syndrome." I am changing your name to But-Why.

GH:

I don't like that.

Gary:

You don't like that one? Well, when you are being the anti-you, But-Why is your name.

GH:

I go through periods where I am really happy and life's great, and then I go to "But what's the point?"

Gary:

Who does that belong to?

GH:

Well, not me but...

Gary:

Yeah, not me *but*... But-Why.

GH:

I would like to stay up there for longer. You know what I mean?

Gary:

Well then, stay there. You are working extra hard to keep the limitations and lies in place. What if you just gave those up?

GH:

I know I am not depressed. But I don't see the reason. I look out at those mountains and I think of dances with wolves...

Gary:

You just want to go off in the wilderness by yourself and dance with wolves?

GH:

Yeah, but then I'd have to come back.

Gary:

Are you sure your name isn't But-Why? You just said, "But why?" five times.

GH:

So our life and our purpose... I get caught up in all of that stuff, you know what I mean?

Gary:

Yeah, that's the human reality of purpose.

GH:

And what is your reality of purpose?

Gary:

To have a good time. To enjoy living. To look at the stars and see them twinkling in the sky. To look at the rainbows and see the beauty in them. To look at the grass and say, "Oh my God, look at it grow."

Instead of looking at the gift, you are going to "But why?" You guys want to POD and POC everything and suddenly be different. The thing is you have to have the practice of being a phenomenance. You have to practice at it, not assume that it is just going to show up. Have you practiced being happy? No. You are not practicing the joy of being. You need to practice. You are trying to find the practicality of everything, which is why you are using your doubt, your limitations, and your lies. You are using those to determine what your choice is rather than asking:

+ How can I practice to be happy?
+ What practice could I put into place to be happy?

You have to practice being a phenomenance.

You have to practice, folks. You don't know how to do this. You don't know how to be the phenomenance you actually are. You don't know how to function without this reality. I am trying to get you to the place where you have the phenomenance that places you outside of this reality, beyond this reality, which gives you a choice for something others will never, ever be able to choose. They will never be able to choose it. Why? Because the only phenomenance they have in their life is their misery. Everything about this reality is the phenomenance of lies, judgments, limitations, and feelings. "My feelings are..." I love that one. The other one I love is "My experience tells me..." Your experience is a crock of shit that you made happen. Your experience is a creation. It's not a frigging experience. You chose to create that for what reason? Get over it. Move on. Create something!

You have to practice, all of you, to create a life. Ask: "What could I put into existence today to start creating my own reality and my own life?" You keep looking at "Why?" and "What's the value?" and "What's the purpose?" and "Why do I do this?" and that's not getting you anywhere. You need to ask: "What could I practice today that would give me the reality and the life that I'd really like to have that I have not been willing to choose?"

Somewhere deep down inside you, or far out in the universe where you threw it, there is something you know about what you would like to have and what you'd like to be and what you would like to do. Otherwise you wouldn't be here. You would not have come to this class unless you knew there was something more that you wanted that you have not yet chosen. You keep trying to look for *why* you don't choose it. I keep trying to show you *how* to choose it.

GH:

Why am I obsessed with *why?*

Gary:

Because you're a whiner: "Why, why, why?"

GH:

How can all of you live and not want to know the reason?

Gary:

You're assuming there's a reason for doing things. There is no reason. People just choose.

GH:

The reason for life, living. It is just to have fun?

Gary:

There is no reason for life. What's the reason for life to a horse or a cow or a pig?

GH:

They're just happy, being a pig or a cow or a horse.

Gary:

Yeah! The happiest thing we could do is give you a lobotomy. Here's the thing: If you choose for happiness and you practice happiness, you will get happiness. Practice giving up doubt and trying to figure out what you would like to create in your life. Ask: "What could I do today that would be fun for me right away?" Just that question. Then you won't go to "Oh, I don't want to do…" "I don't want to create…" "I don't want to…" "Why do I have to…?"

PRACTICE AND PLAY

LY:

Anytime the word *practice* is mentioned I go "Eww."

Gary:

Did your parents make you practice an instrument or something?

LY:

They tried to, but I refused.

Gary:

When I say *practice*, I mean start doing the elements of what's going to create what you want. You say, "I want this." You want it, you want it to be delivered to you, you want me to POD and POC it onto your plate, but you don't ask, "What would I have to do to get this?"

I'm going to change the word *practice* now, just for you. You play and that's your practice. Ask:

+ How could I play with this today to get a result?
+ What can I play with here that would create more than I ever thought possible?

LY:

I like that.

If you choose for happiness and you practice happiness,
you will get happiness.

STEPPING INTO PHENOMENANCE

DT:

You said that phenomenance is about stepping into it. You have been running processes to do with the phenomenance of being you, the phenomenance of money, and so on. Do we have to step into every single phenomenance?

Gary:

Yes, you have to step into each one, which is why I said you have to practice. Ask: "What kind of phenomenance of money could I practice today?" Or if you're LY, you ask: "What kind of phenomenance of money could I *play* with today?"

DT:

When you say *practice*, do you mean stepping into it?

Gary:

I mean trying it out for size. If you want to learn to dance, don't you have to practice dancing? My youngest daughter had the point of view that she always had to take private lessons before she took group lessons because she wanted to be better than everybody else before she started. That was her point of view: "I want to be better than everybody else before I start." That's not a wrongness; it's just the point of view she was functioning from. She chose to do whatever it took to be better before she started. What if you did that?

If you want to learn to dance,
don't you have to practice dancing?

LIFE IS A CELEBRATION

After I got divorced, I moved into a small apartment. I took one set of china out of the four sets we had, one set of sterling silver flatware out of four, the pots and pans that had belonged to my parents, and an old set of "everyday" dishes. I put the twenty-piece set of china in a closet, thinking, "I'll put this away for a special occasion." Then I said, "Wait! What the hell am I talking about? I'm not going to have a dinner party for twenty people in this little apartment." So I put all the good china in the kitchen cupboard, I put the sterling silver flatware in the silverware drawer, and I ate off china plates and sterling silver flatware that had a replacement cost of $60 apiece. I said, "I'm not going to do a big dinner party, so I'd better enjoy today, because today is all I've got." Why is your life not a celebration today?

My reality is that life should be a celebration every day, not just on special occasions. You should dress well every day, not just on special occasions. You should choose to have beauty in your life not just on special occasions, but every day.

You are the only one who can receive from you to the degree that you can give to you. And in so doing, you make your life a celebration every day. I don't neglect saying to people what I want them to hear. I don't stop myself from enjoying myself. I drink what I want, I eat what I want, and I do whatever is going to work for me. If you are not willing to have fun, you will never choose something that is fun for you.

If you aren't celebrating life, why are you living? If you are celebrating your life, you are celebrating the living on planet Earth. And if you give that, the Earth gets better.

The phenomenance of living is the celebration of living.

What have you made so vital about never possessing the phenomenance of living that keeps life as not a celebration? Everything that is times a godzillion, will you destroy and uncreate it all? Right and Wrong, Good and Bad, POD and POC, All 9, Shorts, Boys, and Beyonds.

The phenomenance of living is the celebration of living.

SHARE YOUR BEAUTY AND YOUR TALENTS

Gary:

NM, it was very nice to hear you playing the piano this morning.

NM:

Thank you.

Gary:

That was a compliment! You received it like it was shit. When you play the piano, you are stunning. Why do you not see that it is a gift you have to give to the world?

NM:

I have a really different point of view. I have to sit with your compliment and receive it and allow it.

Gary:

You have to allow it and say, "Wow, how does it get any better than this?" How it gets any better is you playing more. You have a gift. You have a talent. Why are you not giving it to the world? Do you have a piano at home?

NM:

I have the possibility of getting a piano, a beautiful one.

Gary:

"I have the possibility of getting a piano" is not "I have a piano at home." That is not a *yes*. Get a frigging piano and get it now. I don't care what it costs you. I don't care what it takes. Get that piano and play it all the time. And open the doors and windows and let the neighbors hear it.

If you want more in your life, NM, start sharing your ability. I was stunned when I heard you play. It was so beautiful. Why are you not playing the piano all the time? Any time you see an empty piano, you should play it, because that is honoring the piano. Pianos get out of tune because people don't play them. Don't just play for special occasions. It is part of the gift you have to add to your life, to LM's life, and to the life of everybody around you. That is a blessed possibility.

NM:

Thank you.

"I'd better enjoy today, because today is all I've got."

Gary:

You have to share your beauty. MA started sharing her beauty and it has been really nice for a lot of us guys and a few of the women. I used to watch her walk into a room and I would ask "What is she hiding for?" MA, as you have come out of cover, haven't you had a better life?

MA:

Yes!

Gary:

Ladies, dress up and be as beautiful as you can be every day. Because you know what? That's a gift to people, too. What if every day was the party? Are you dressing for the party? One thing I loved about the past was that people dressed up all the time. They had their day dresses, they had their evening dresses, and they didn't do their "scruffies." There was no scruffy.

Why aren't all of you sharing your beauty and your talents? You will share your misery but you won't share your beauty. When you have these talents, why the hell are you not sharing them? They are a blessed possibility.

MA:

Yes!

KC:

When you were talking to NM about playing the piano, you told her she should play all the time. You said, "Don't wait for an event." When I heard that, I thought, "You are the event." It is like using your sterling silver every day, not just for special occasions.

Gary:

If I am alive, it's a special event. If I wake up this morning, it's a special day. I'd better frigging celebrate, which is why I will sometimes have champagne and caviar as my dinner. Or champagne and pancakes. Or champagne and pie. It doesn't have to make sense. It has to be a celebration of the moment. When you celebrate in the moment, your body will say, "I want this." And when you give it that, it's "Oh my God! That tastes good," not "I shouldn't be eating this because it's not politically correct." My personal point of view is that champagne is one of the food groups of life.

If you are celebrating your life, you are celebrating the living on planet Earth.
And if you give that, the Earth gets better.

WHAT'S POSSIBLE BEYOND THIS REALITY?

Close your eyes for a minute. I want you to look at the reality you have available that you have never chosen. The universe you have never chosen. Are you beginning to feel that? How big is it? Okay, good. Now be unhappy. (It seems a little irrelevant, doesn't it?) What reality, what universe is available to you that you have not chosen that if you choose it will create a different reality on planet Earth? And how big is that?

You have been taught your entire life that unhappiness is the greatest relevance there is. People say to you, "You're unhappy, what's wrong with you? How can I help you? Can

I give you a pill? Can I stop your unhappiness?" What they don't ask you is "What's possible beyond this reality?"

What is possible beyond this reality and this universe that you have available to you that you have not yet chosen? Everything that doesn't allow you to choose it, will you destroy and uncreate it all? Right and Wrong, Good and Bad, POD and POC, All 9, Shorts, Boys, and Beyonds.

Being unhappy doesn't seem like it's your best choice, does it? Everything that is times a godzillion, will you destroy and uncreate it all? Right and Wrong, Good and Bad, POD and POC, All 9, Shorts, Boys, and Beyonds.

You've got to be willing to be happy, whether or not anybody else is. It's easier to walk through the world happy, expansive, joyful, and present as you whether anybody else receives it or not.

*What reality, what universe is available to you
that you have not chosen that if you choose it will
create a different reality on planet Earth?*

Lies, Judgments, and Limitations

Gary:

Dain and I were talking this morning, and I became aware of the fact that the one place you are willing to institute phenomenance is in the areas of lies, judgments, and limitations. When I talk about phenomenance in any area of your life, you say, "Well, I don't know…" but you will phenomenally accept a lie. You will phenomenally accept a judgment. You will phenomenally accept a limitation.

THE SEDUCTION OF LIMITATION

The seduction of limitation is that it is very slowly but surely induced into your reality through very subtle moments, methods, and awarenesses. Nobody talks about the energetics of the limitations that are impelled at us daily, continuously, constantly. It is not something people look at.

You choose a limitation because you believe the level of possibility is too extreme for you to have. You think it's not okay for you to have it.

ST:

You have said that behind every limitation is a possibility. Could you explain this, please?

Gary:

Let's say you have a bunch of pigs on your farm and you decide, "I can't keep all of these pigs. It's too much work." Then do you go to "I have to give my pigs away or kill them"? Or do you say, "Oh! I could get on the internet and sell them"?

ST:

Sell them.

Gary:

And how long would that take?

ST:

Half an hour.

Gary:

Yes, because behind every limitation of having pigs is a possibility you haven't considered yet. Usually the possibility is so extreme that you don't want to know it and you go back to the limitation.

ST:

So if we just ask, "What else is possible?" that can open the possibility?

Gary:

Yes, you just have to ask:

+ What else is possible here?
+ What else is possible that I haven't considered?

*The seduction of limitation is that it is very slowly
but surely induced into your reality through very
subtle moments, methods, and awarenesses.*

YOU AVOID POSSIBILITIES EVERY TIME YOU COME TO A CONCLUSION

Most of the time, you avoid possibilities. Is that at all real to you? You especially avoid possibilities every time you come to a conclusion.

How many conclusions are you using to avoid the possibilities you could be choosing? Everything that is times a godzillion, will you destroy and uncreate it all? Right and Wrong, Good and Bad, POD and POC, All 9, Shorts, Boys, and Beyonds.

What conclusion are you using to avoid the possibilities you could be choosing? "I need to control" is a conclusion. It's not a possibility. Everything that is times a godzillion, will you destroy and uncreate it all? Right and Wrong, Good and Bad, POD and POC, All 9, Shorts, Boys and Beyonds.

If you decide, "I don't want to pay for this for this person" is that a conclusion? Yes. Does that avoid any possibilities? Yes, thousands. Why? Because that one conclusion, that one decision, that one belief, that one judgment, holds down anything that could not fit the reality of what you have available. It can only fit the reality of your conclusion.

Anytime you make a judgment, a decision, a computation, or a conclusion, nothing that does not match it can come into your awareness or your life.

What conclusion are you using to avoid the possibilities you could be choosing? Everything that is times a godzillion, will you destroy and uncreate it all? Right and Wrong, Good and Bad, POD and POC, All 9, Shorts, Boys, and Beyonds.

Have you come to enough conclusions to make sure you are not making half a million dollars a year or more? Everything that is times a godzillion, will you destroy and uncreate it all? Right and Wrong, Good and Bad, POD and POC, All 9, Shorts, Boys, and Beyonds.

What conclusions are you using to avoid the possibilities you could be choosing? Everything that is times a godzillion, will you destroy and uncreate it all? Right and Wrong, Good and Bad, POD and POC, All 9, Shorts, Boys, and Beyonds.

"How many conclusions are you using to avoid the possibilities you could be choosing?"

JUDGMENT DESTROYS ALL CONNECTIONS

You've got to get to the awareness that judgment in any form is not real, and it is destructive if you make it real, vital, and important. When you have no judgment, when you have a reality in which judgment does not exist, other people can give you their judgment and you'll say, "Oh, okay." It won't be real, vital, or important.

ES: I have been trying to handle or understand judgment, and I see that I have been making judgment real. I see how much separation it creates among people.

Gary:

That's what judgment does—it destroys all connections. You can't have any kind of communion with somebody in the face of judgment.

ES:

That is so clear to me for the first time.

Gary:

That's one of the reasons Dain and I have the kind of connection and communion we have. It is not based on normal relationship; it's based on the fact that he gave up his willingness to judge me—and I don't judge him. So what he chooses is what he chooses, whether I agree with it or not, whether I think it is a good idea or not.

Judgment is not part of my reality, so I have to be in question. When judgment is part of your reality, you give up questioning, and when you give up questioning, you give up creation. When you give up questioning, you give up possibilities. So no judgment might be in your best interest. But it is your reality and your choice. You need to choose what's going to work for you.

INTERESTING POINT OF VIEW

NM:

How do I get rid of every judgment in my universe?

Gary:

Every time a judgment comes up, say: "Interesting point of view, I have that point of view," and "Everywhere I did that or was that, POD and POC it."

NM:

There is no real fast way?

Gary:

That is the fast way. You have taken four trillion years to get to the point where you are finally willing to choose something greater. You have been doing Access for a couple of years. What's the fast way?

NM:

This way is the fast way.

Gary:

When I first learned that judgment was a way to destroy everything I said, "Enough! I am not doing judgment. I don't care what it takes. My reality will not include judgment. Period." Every time I had a point of view, I said, "Interesting point of view, I have this point of view." I did that for six months.

If I judged myself, I would say, "Interesting point of view." If I judged somebody else, I'd say, "Interesting point of view."

Then I learned the tool, "If I am judging, it is because I have been there and done that. So everywhere I did that and was that, I POD and POC it." And then it would go away.

DW:

And if I am judging myself...

Gary:

It means you are doing as much self-loathing as you can so you can diminish you, so you can keep yourself pathetic and small, so that you never have the life or reality that gives you all.

DW:

And at the same time if someone else is judging you, you are making the judgment real.

Gary:

The purpose of judgment is to destroy. Why would somebody judge you? To destroy you. Why would they try to destroy you? Because somehow you are greater than they are, and they are afraid of you. People only judge those they are afraid of.

When judgment is part of your reality, you give up questioning, and when you give up questioning, you give up creation. When you give up questioning, you give up possibilities.

"NO POINT OF VIEW IS ACTUALLY MINE"

MP:

I am so frigging aware that I am picking up everybody else's reality and calling it my own reality.

Gary:

That's the reason you've got to use "Interesting point of view, I have this point of view" for every point of view you have for six months. You will begin to realize, "Wow, no point of view is actually mine. I am aware of everything." Now if you could be aware of everything, would that be more fun?

You guys want the magic wand that goes "Boogedy, boogedy, boo! You are free and true." Try using "Interesting point of view."

"Wow, no point of view is actually mine.
I am aware of everything."
If you could be aware of everything, would that be more fun?

THE WILLINGNESS TO BE JUDGED

ND:

I realized that I attempted to avoid being judged by living up to my mother's and other people's realities and by being so good that nobody could ever judge me as bad or wrong. That is totally judgment! I also realized how much my family's reality is "Don't do!" Anytime I would do something, I would get judged by them. The only way to not get judged was to not do. Just be still. Just be frozen and you don't get judged.

You once asked me, "Are you willing to be judged?" and I saw that I can't have the willingness to be judged unless I am willing to be without judgment of myself. I want to say, "Thank you," Gary, because this has opened a space that has never been there before.

MN:

I have gotten to that over the past few years. Gary, you and Dain have taught me that. But I get the energy of where people are choosing to function from, and it's quite intense.

Gary:

Just because it's intense doesn't mean it's real. It doesn't mean you have to go to the judgment "This is so real. This is awful. These poor people." I look at them and say, "Wow, interesting point of view."

JUDGMENT VS. AWARENESS

JT:

I recently dated somebody who is ninety-eight percent evil and two percent nice.

Gary:

You will always see the two percent nice before you see the ninety-eight percent evil. And you will assume that you are responsible for their choosing the evil because you have dedicated your life to seeing the good in people. Your reality is "I will see the good."

Dain:

Even if it's not there.

Gary:

Even if it's not there. Good point, Dain. That of course doesn't apply to any of the rest of you, right? Yeah, it does! Most of you have the utopian ideal, "I always see the good in people. All people are basically good." It's a judgment that all people are good. It's not an awareness. It's a conclusion and a judgment.

JT:

That links into expecting somebody...

Gary:

To be good. And expecting the goodness to show up. And when the goodness doesn't show up, you assume you are somehow at fault.

JT:

So it is about letting go of the expectations?

Gary:

Yes. When I learned that projections, expectations, separations, judgments, and rejections are the way people function in the world I said, "Any place I am doing that, POD and POC it. That's not going to be part of my reality." I will not do projection or expectation on anyone because I know that all it does is lock them into proving me right or proving me wrong and then they have no choice. I'm not interested in that.

You are stuck with so diligently wanting to see the good in people that you eliminate your willingness to see the place where they will do evil. Ninety-eight percent is bad and two percent is good, and yet the only part you will focus on is the good. Who does that hurt?

JT:

Me.

Gary:

Why would you want to hurt you that much? I am willing to see people for exactly who and what they are. I have no projections or expectations. I have no rejections. I don't have any point of view about them except "Oh, this is cute. This is your point of view. This is what you are going to choose. Okay fine." If they change, fine, and if they don't change, no problem.

You never see where people won't change. That's killing you. You always expect the good and project the good. "All people are wonderful." Nope, some people are jerks. Some are good, some are kind, some are great—but most aren't. When you try to only see the good in people and you dedicate your life to seeing only the good, you are cutting off your awareness, and it will backfire on you every time. That's the reason you get disappointed by people.

JT:

I feel like you just destroyed my whole reality by saying that people aren't good.

Gary Douglas

Gary:

They aren't! I know a nice, kind man. His Christian business partner cheated him out of $20 million. He still thinks the guy who cheated him is a good guy because he's a Christian.

JT:

I could probably relate to that.

Gary:

The guy took my friend for $20 million. That's really a good person, right? You've got to look and see the person. "Okay, this person is insane. This person is mean. This person is exactly what he is. This person is fat. This person is ugly. This person is old. This person is…."

You end up judging you instead of somebody else. That doesn't work because it's cutting off your awareness of what people will do. One of the must-haves in my reality is "I will never function from unawareness." And when I do, I say, "Oh damn, I did it again. Well, enough of that. I'll have more awareness in this area." That is where you have to choose your reality. You're trying to choose a reality in which everything turns out beautiful. How's that working for you? You had a guy next door who used you. You saw the goodness in him.

JT:

Yeah, because he's a nice guy.

Gary:

No, he isn't a nice guy! He's a jerk who used you. VT, you see that guy as he is.

VT:

Yes, and sometimes when JT and I have conflicts, I say, "That's how this person is," and she says, "You can't make that judgment of them."

Gary:

It's not a judgment. It's an observation. JT, you have judgments of the goodness of people.

You judge people as good when they are actually not. That's a judgment. That's not an awareness.

When you try to only see the good in people and you dedicate your life to seeing only the good, you are cutting off your awareness, and it will backfire on you every time.

CUTTING PEOPLE OUT OF YOUR LIFE

VT:

I have realized I've got default mechanisms set in, so I will cut people out of my life without even realizing it.

Gary:

Well that's kind of cool. The only part that's a lie is "without even realizing it."

VT:

I would like to change that. I would like to move beyond that and be more like you and not have to cut people out.

Gary:

Do you want to cut people out?

VT:

No, it just kind of occurs or happens.

Gary:

It doesn't just "kind of occur" It is what you choose. You choose to cut people out before they cut you out. How much judgment do you have to have of you to make that a reality?

VT:

A hell of a lot.

Gary:

Yeah. And that's why you do it. You have a judgment that somehow people will cut you out. There are a few people in Access who like you, but we already know they're idiots, so you should cut them out.

VT:

What can I choose or what can I do differently?

Gary:

It's not about *doing* something differently. It's "What can I *be* different that would create a different reality for me?" You've got to look at it and say: "I would like to create a different reality here. This constant state of cutting people out and not acknowledging what they are to me and not acknowledging them is crazy. I'm not going to do that anymore."

VT:

I'm not going to do that anymore.

Gary:

Okay, and you have to say, "I'm not going to judge me anymore either."

VT:

I am not going to judge me anymore either.

Gary:

You just lied to me.

VT:

That's a massive one for me because I judge myself all the time.

Gary:

Yes, I know. Total judgment.

VT:

I am ready to choose something different.

Gary:

Then choose it. Look at what you want.

What have you made so vital about never possessing the phenomenance of total change that keeps you in the judgment, the limitation, and the smallness of you for all eternity? Everything that is times a godzillion, will you destroy and uncreate it all? Right and Wrong, Good and Bad, POD and POC, All 9, Shorts, Boys, and Beyonds.

ACCUSATION

KC:

You have said that if somebody accuses you of something, it is what they themselves are doing. How do you receive the energy of accusation? Sometimes it comes quite forcefully.

Gary:

My point of view is that the accusation is an interesting point of view. I say, "Thank you for exposing you." I consider it a gift when somebody accuses me. Then I get to know exactly what they are doing.

KC:

When someone accuses me, I contract.

Gary:

Yes, you withdraw from it. You try to pretend it isn't really occurring. You believe that if you can withstand the hideousness of their judgment, someday they will change. You have the point of view that if you're nice enough, long enough, people will change. Those are utopian ideals.

What do you want to create as your reality? I looked at my life and I said, "I have been creating a place where I expect things of people and they never deliver. I've been creating my life from the point of view of "I can get along without anyone" and then I realized that "anyone" included me. It's hard to get along without you in your own life. I realized that I needed to make it so that my life counted to me, not anybody else. I want to know at the end of my life that I was happy with it. I want to know that I have done something that pleases me so much that I will be glad that I was here on planet Earth. It's not about making other people happy with me. It's about making me happy with me.

Are you making you happy with you? Or are you trying to make other people happy? If you don't have the joy of you in your life, you don't actually have a life. You're creating a reality based on somebody else's point of view about you. Please don't do that. You are denying the world the gift you actually are. *What* that gift is I don't *know.* *That* the gift is, I do know.

Are you making you happy with you? Or are you trying to make other people happy?
If you don't have the joy of you in your life, you don't actually have a life.

"HELPING"

ND:

It's clear to me that part of my reality is helping others to know theirs.

Gary:

If you are trying to help, you have to judge everything you do or don't do and everything others receive or don't receive, which gives you how much freedom to be? None! To help is to be superior. If you have no judgment, can you be superior?

ND:

No.

Gary:

Can you create a different kind of possibility?

ND:

Yes.

Gary:

Part of my reality is to honor the gift that each person is in my life, and the only way to do that is by having no judgment. Each person is a gift in their own right and in their own way. No matter how crazy they are, no matter how insane they are, no matter how stupid they are, they are still a gift. And when you get that, you can't, won't, and don't judge anyone. You will just receive them and know that all you object to about them is where you are being them. The only reason you object to anybody is because you are being them. Otherwise you wouldn't object to them.

You have to get to the place where there is no judgment or conclusion in your life. You have to make the demand, "My reality will be without judgment and without conclusion."

ND:

Can we have a clearing for that?

Gary:

No, it's a choice and a demand you have to make of yourself. Ultimately choice dominates all clearings.

ND:

And then constantly doing "Interesting point of view," because so many of the judgments I am aware of aren't mine.

Gary:

If you are constantly doing "Interesting point of view," eventually you get to the point where you *are* interesting point of view and you don't come to conclusion about anything. But you've got to commit to having a reality in which there is no judgment and no conclusion. Conclusion is nothing more than a judgment solidified to make you right.

ND:

I commit.

> *Part of my reality is to honor the gift that*
> *each person is in my life, and the only way*
> *to do that is by having no judgment.*

THE ABILITY TO CHANGE

The phenomenance of you is the ability to change. You may not realize it, but one of the things you came here to do in this lifetime is to change reality. To do that, you have to be the inspiration. You also have to be the perspiration that never gives up, that never says *no*, that never says *quit*. You always know you're going to create more regardless of anybody else's point of view. You make a place in you where you say, "You know what? I'm not having this anymore. I'm not going to live with the judgment."

It's not "I can live with the judgment," it's not "I can handle the judgment," it's not "I can deal with the judgment." It's "Judgment is not going to be part of my reality." When you function from no judgment as your reality, you change.

When you function from no judgment as your reality, you change everyone that comes in contact with you.

PR:

Besides the demand of not having judgment as part of your reality, what else is required?

Gary:

That's it.

PR:

That's it?

Gary:

That's it. Every time you find yourself doing judgment, you say:

- Okay, whoever's point of view this is, return to sender.
- Everything about that I thought was mine, POD and POC that.
- And by the way, I'm not doing judgment anymore. Get out of my head!

PR:

I love that! Thank you.

When you function from no judgment as your reality, you change everyone that comes in contact with you.

"Saving" People

BUYING INTO OTHER PEOPLE'S SUFFERING

PA:

My husband has fractures in his neck, and he chooses to go out and drink. He always falls down when he drinks, and there is a good chance, with these fractures, that he is going to kill himself. Sometimes I buy into the sadness of this. That's being controlled, isn't it?

Gary:

You are buying into the suffering as though it is real. That's part of the lies, judgments, and limitations of this reality. The level of phenomenance you guys have at making that stuff real is quite extraordinary—because it's not actually real. It is just an interesting point of view. It's not right, it's not wrong, it's not anything. It's just a choice.

If he fell down and killed himself, you could be happy that he found a quick way out. He broke his neck and now he can go out and get drunk and break it totally. Or he could be so crippled he could only use his mind.

PA:

I would love to get to be happy around that. That he could be so crippled.

Gary:

Well, why wouldn't you be happy for him being able to choose so brilliantly? Are you still trying to save him?

PA:

I guess I must be.

Gary:

What is the relevance of saving the people you love instead of empowering them?

What have you made so vital about saving the people you love instead of empowering them? Everything that is times a godzillion, will you destroy and uncreate it all? Right and Wrong, Good and Bad, POD and POC, All 9, Shorts, Boys, and Beyonds.

Why don't you get totally caring and say, "Honey, if this is what you want to choose, then go for it"?

Everything you have done to save the ones you love and the ones you don't love and the stupids and the crazies and the not-so-brights and the half-wits and the whole-wits and the completely-wits and the wit-less, will you destroy and uncreate all that? Right and Wrong, Good and Bad, POD and POC, All 9, Shorts, Boys, and Beyonds.

PA:

So what I keep sticking myself with is…

Gary:

You care for the man. Are you kidding? I care for the man too, but I am willing to let him die.

PA:

I am willing to let him die if he would stop torturing me with all of his suffering.

Gary:

Yes, but what's the purpose of suffering?

PA:

I didn't think that there was a purpose.

Gary:

The purpose of suffering is to torture others. It's the most dynamic manipulation on the planet. "I'm suffering. I have cancer. I am going to die in two years. Give me everything I want."

I say, "Well, if you are dying, have a good trip."

PA:

He is choosing against himself.

Gary:

That's a choice people have. He is choosing the anti-him. It is a choice he has. It is easier for him to choose against himself than it is to choose him. As long as he is choosing the anti-him, he can control by his point of view. He's got two sons and a wife that are about as controllable as the wind.

PA:

I am wondering what it would take for me to give up believing that he really can't see a different possibility.

Gary:

It doesn't matter whether he can see a different possibility. The reality is he is not choosing a different possibility.

PA:

That is true. He is not choosing a different possibility.

Gary:

You and your boys would choose a different possibility for him in a heartbeat, but you cannot overcome the mechanisms that control him. Even if you were all on the same page, fighting like hell, he'd still go against you. And can I just say that you and your sons are stronger in the area of not being controlled than any other three people I have ever known in my life?

PA:

And yet we are still letting this guy control us.

Gary:

No, you are trying to save him. You care for him. You love him. And of course you think you want to save him. But the question you are not asking is "Does he want to be saved? Does he really want to be saved?" As long as you keep trying to save his ass, he is going to try and control the situation by dying on his own command. What if you gave in and said, "Oh well, if you want to go, goodbye. It has been fun. Thanks for being my dad. Thanks for being my husband. We'll see you in the afterlife."

What have you made so vital about saving the people you love that destroys you in the process? Everything that is times a godzillion, will you destroy and uncreate it all? Right and Wrong, Good and Bad, POD and POC, All 9, Shorts, Boys, and Beyonds.

NJ:

That tool Gary is giving about not saving people really works. My mother has been committing slow suicide for a while.

Gary:

She has been playing pathetic for about six years now.

NJ:

Any time there is any disruption in the family, she gets worse, so I asked her what she's creating with that. She realized she was trying to bring the family back together and get them all to care about each other instead of fighting. I asked her, "Are you sure that is going to work?"

She asked, "What do you mean?"

I said "Well, it might backfire on you. They might decide that you are too hard to look after, put you in a home, and sell the house."

Gary:

Telling her that she is going to be put in a home would make her say, "No, I am not leaving my house. Nobody gets my house until I am dead."

NJ:

That is exactly what happened. She stopped immediately.

Gary:

Well done! That's wonderful.

> *What is the relevance of saving the people*
> *you love instead of empowering them?*

MAKING YOURSELF THE GOD OR GODDESS OF SOMEBODY ELSE'S REALITY

HB:

There is something liberating and freeing when you say, "Don't save people. Empower them." Can we talk some more about the idea of saving people? This has been one of the biggest things that lock me up. There have been a couple of people that I have been more invested in than others, and when I get invested in them, I lose a sense of possibility and the joy of forward movement.

Gary:

What have you made so vital about saving NK that keeps you from creating everything that you are capable of? I am using NK because he represents the same energy of the people you care about that you are trying to save.

HB:

Exactly.

Gary:

The moment you decide you've got to save somebody, you stop creating.

HB:

That must be what feels so wonky about it.

Gary:

The moment you try to save somebody, you've decided how the world should be and everything has to be adjusted according to that reality—except the universe doesn't necessarily agree with you.

HB:

Wow! No shit. NK has a very different point of view about what he should do.

Gary:

"And he should do what I want because I am goddess!"

HB:

Right! Thanks to you and Dain, I am more willing to be in allowance and recognize that I can't always see what's great. I can't always see what's going to create the greatness that's coming.

Gary:

Yes, but you can have an awareness of it, and if you give up your point of view about what it is, it will happen more easily.

HB:

I have seen that in action, and yet I still won't fully go to that knowing.

Gary:

Yes, I said you were a goddess intentionally. When you try to make you the god or goddess of somebody else's reality, you stop the creation of possibility.

Everywhere you have made you the god or goddess of somebody else's reality, will you destroy and uncreate all that? Right and Wrong, Good and Bad, POD and POC, All 9, Shorts, Boys, and Beyonds.

"WHERE IS THIS CHOICE GOING TO LEAD ME?"

HB:

There is something else here. There's a weird gray area between knowing the energy of possibility...

Gary:

It is not a gray area. It's black and white. You know what is possible and instead of choosing what is possible, you try to create something that is going to get a result. You have already decided what the result is. You have not questioned whether it is a greater result or a lesser result. You have not asked, "Where is this going to lead me?" I keep telling you to ask, "Where is this choice going to lead me?" You have to be willing to be led. You're not willing to be led; you are only interested in being followed.

Everywhere you have decided you want to be followed instead of being led, will you destroy and uncreate it all? Right and Wrong, Good and Bad, POD and POC, All 9, Shorts, Boys, and Beyonds.

HB:

I am actually willing to be led quite a lot in business—but not in personal relationships. Or when I am lost in a city, I will say, "Help me!" and I will know to go around a corner. I am led like that all the time.

Gary:

Yes, but why aren't you led like that in your personal relationships?

HB:

Is it a control thing?

Gary:

Yeah. You want to be a god or goddess. What have you made so vital about being the god or goddess of your own reality that keeps you from what will lead you to a different reality?

HB:

That must be the expression of false power.

Gary:

It is what has been defined as power in this reality. In this reality, power is always defined as control over others. But true power is the willingness to see that you are being led by something and you have no idea why you are being led there.

When Dain and I moved to Texas, I knew I was being led there. The justification for moving was "I'll get to see Xander more." Great justification. Do I get to see him more? Not really, because I am never home. I got to see him more when he would come to visit me in California. But I justified moving like crazy, knowing we had to move there. Then once we got there, I went looking for a new bookkeeper and that led me to an accountant, who led me to a lawyer, and now because of that lawyer, we have the international Access Company, which is what I had been shooting for forever, but nobody could ever tell me how to get there. For five years, I had been trying to figure out how to create that and nobody could tell me anything. Nobody I talked to knew enough to tell me where to go or what to do.

It was the same with the Antique Guild. I have three containers of things that are about to arrive in Australia. I just got the information about how much money it is going to cost me to ship them. I was not prepared to spend $30,000 at this time, but somehow I am going to come up with it. The thing is that I am willing to follow the lead of it. I ask:

+ Do I really need to do this now?
+ Could I do it another time?
+ Why am I doing this?
+ Why am I doing this business at all?

But I also ask, "Do it? Not do it? Do it. Okay, good." It is as simple as that if you are willing to follow the awareness that is innately greater than your time span of reality. You have to follow the awareness that is greater than your time span of reality because most of you don't have a time span of reality greater than two years.

HB:

Can we bring this back to people again? Because you are talking about projects and business.

Gary:

The same thing applies with people if you're not willing to see. You are willing to see "I can be with NK for two years." But at the same time you have to ask, "Could I be with this person for fifty years?"

HB:

I have never thought that.

Gary:

Yes, I know but you have to ask, "What would lead me to having this person in my life on a continuous basis?"

RECEIVING THE GIFT

HB:

I have noticed a similar energy with my birth father, my brothers, and NK. Those are the strongest ones. It is similar to what PA was bringing up about watching her husband die.

Gary:

Impending doom.

HB:

Yeah. Impending doom. I was trying to avoid saying that, but that's what it is.

Gary:

You won't follow where it is going to lead you because you don't have the willingness to trust that you would never choose wrong.

HB:

Can we talk about that in terms of my birth father, for example?

Gary:

Did you choose him as the correct father for you?

HB:

Of course, I must have.

Gary:

You keep trying to see how he did things to you or how he was bad or how he wasn't bad. Instead, you could ask: "What did I get out of this? I got someone as a father that I don't have to care about and who doesn't care for me."

HB:

But I don't see those as positive things like you do!

Gary:

Why?

HB:

I don't have an answer for you. I don't see that as liberation, as in "Oh, I don't have to care for that person, thank God." Because I do care for that person!

Gary:

You just stunned me. I just got a level of awareness of me that's different than I've ever had before.

HB:

You say how great it is that you don't have to care. I can't relate to what you are relating to.

Gary:

Wow. Okay. Sorry you've got to give me a moment. Wow.

HB:

I don't see that as the silver lining like you do.

Gary:

Wow. One of the foundations of my reality just got changed. I don't think Rescue Remedy is going to help. I don't think champagne is going to work, either. I have to readjust a few billion things. I never realized that for me, freedom is the recognition of what you *don't have to do.* For you, freedom is getting away from what you have decided you *have to do.* You have no choice. I have no need.

HB:

I don't feel like I have a choice about what happened with my birth father. I feel like I didn't have a choice with any of that. It was just done. It was never "Wow, thank God

I have the freedom to not need this man." That has never crossed my mind. That choice is not something that is super-available to me.

Gary:

It's not available at all. But you would like to have freedom from the influence that he was in your life.

HB:

Yes, that is true.

Gary:

But you can't have that—unless you are willing to get the gift it is. You've got to get that somebody who doesn't need you and doesn't want you, somebody who doesn't require your feedback, your help, or anything else, is giving you a gift. That's the gift he's giving you. He gave you freedom from him by not wanting to be there for you. You don't see it that way.

I never understood why you didn't see the gift of this. That's because you don't believe in gifts. You don't believe that what people do to you is the gift they are giving. You think it's the wrongness or the badness. I am glad I am sitting down.

HB:

What you are offering seems more like a coping mechanism than a freedom. I am being honest with you right now.

Gary:

And forceful.

HB:

I can't just agree.

Gary:

I am not asking you to agree.

HB:

I understand.

Gary:

I am trying to see this. I never understood why people choose from this place. I didn't get this innate difference.

HB:

It is also difficult to understand where you are choosing from.

Gary:

Yes, I get that now. I thought mine was really easy.

HB:

It isn't.

Gary:

I thought yours was hard and mine was easy. And now I'm getting "Oh, what is easy for me is not the same as anybody else's point of view."

HB:

Can I please ask some more questions or do we need to come back to this later?

Gary:

I don't have a good answer because I am having a hard time at the moment.

HB:

For the first time, I see a light where I didn't see one before. I don't want to lose this.

Gary:

Okay, I will keep going, but all I want to do is lie down for thirty minutes. I am trying to see the structure you are talking about but not hold in place what was so obvious to me as the gift, so I can get how to commingle these things in some way so that you get greater clarity and I don't have to change. Only kidding about that. I have already changed.

You don't believe that what people do to you is the gift they are giving you.

MN:

The way I am hearing this is that the gift with my mother was her choosing less, not expecting much from me, and looking at me as less-than. That was the gift.

Gary:

Because you never have to live up to her reality.

MN:

Which is actually *down* to her reality.

Gary:

I know, but she considers it *up*. I think part of what is going on for you, HB, is that you keep trying to live up to a reality that is your utopian ideal of what your family should be.

MN:

You always go to the wrongness of you, because that's what was imposed on you. But that which was imposed on you is the wrongness. Like I have been wrong.

Gary:

That's why you can't get the gift of it. What was impelled at you was that you were the wrongness and you had the wrong point of view.

HB:

That's true.

Gary:

You could never receive that the gift they were giving you was that your difference was not a wrongness but a difference they couldn't handle. That's an amazing gift!

HB:

It doesn't feel like a gift. It feels like a total abuse of being.

Gary:

Well, it is an abuse of being because they're judging you. But you are making the phenomenance of judgment greater than the gift of possibility.

HB:

That is exactly where I am stuck. That's exactly true. I make the judgment more valuable than the gift of possibility. Who the hell wants that?

MA:

Gary, you just said that you see it as an empowerment and other people see it as a disservice or an abuse. How do you see it as an empowerment?

Gary:

Because when somebody does disempowerment of you they are not saying "I love you." They are saying, "Go away."

And I say, "Fine, no problem." For me, what is, is. You are looking at some kind of utopian ideal of what ought to be. You're not looking at what is. You think that if you believe strongly enough in their choice for something better, they will choose it.

MA:

So is it just extreme allowance? Is that what it is? You just walk away and you've got other choices?

Gary:

No, it's extreme awareness. For example, your father is choosing to kill himself. For him, killing himself is a gift he is trying to give you. Killing himself is a gift from his point of view, because otherwise, he has to become more abusive in order to control you.

MA:

I saw that as well. Exactly that.

Gary:

You have been willing to see what is. You stopped thinking that if you believed hard enough in something, it would become reality.

HB's mother was so hell-bent on believing that HB needed her father that she forced him to take her, and he was cruel to her. And HB thinks that if she believes strongly enough in him that he will become a loving person. I don't see that as a possible reality.

All of you who decided that it was vital to possess total belief in order to create reality, will you destroy and uncreate all that? Right and Wrong, Good and Bad, POD and POC, All 9, Shorts, Boys, and Beyonds.

TRUE CARING IS ALLOWANCE

Most of you think that caring is saving. I don't have that point of view. For me true caring is recognizing what is. Caring for somebody is recognizing what is. I talked to a friend who was more than upset about the guy he called he his grandson's sperm donor. The guy was lying to his daughter, and my friend wanted to beat the shit out of him. He wanted to make the guy fess up to his lies and deception.

My friend's daughter said, "Dad, I can handle this! Leave him alone. He is not that bad a person."

I said to my friend, "You have just been given walking papers by your daughter. You don't have to try to save her anymore. You need to let her handle this the way she needs to do it."

My friend got it. He said, "Okay, that's it. I'm done." And when he stopped trying to save his daughter, the guy he called the sperm donor started to show up as the asshole he really was.

If you think you have to believe in people to get them to believe in themselves, you are diminishing you and devaluing you and making you a lesser god. You are praying for them, you are believing in them, and you are trying to create reality based on belief rather than seeing what they have chosen as reality. They have chosen the reality they have chosen. It's not good or bad or right or wrong. It is just the reality they have chosen. Somewhere in there, you guys have gotten confused with "If I believe in these people strongly enough, they will change, they will become, they will choose."

I saw in my first wife for thirty minutes an amazing woman, an amazing being. I saw it again a year later for ten minutes, and again a year after that for five minutes, then I saw it for ten seconds about ten times. I thought that if I *believed* strongly enough in her and in the greatness of her, she would eventually choose the greatness. She never did.

Everywhere that all of you are doing that for some stupid person, will you destroy and uncreate it all? Right and Wrong, Good and Bad, POD and POC, All 9, Shorts, Boys, and Beyonds.

When you stop believing, you go to allowance. As long as you have belief, you can't have allowance.

RR:

Does caring come into this conversation? It feels as though what you're talking about is a lot more practical than that.

Gary:

There is "caring," where you try to get people to choose what you would choose—and there is true caring, which is allowance True caring, which is the greatest caring you can give, is allowing somebody to choose whatever they choose. If you are going to have true caring, you've got to have total allowance. It doesn't bother you and it doesn't bother them. They get to have the freedom to be and you get to have the freedom to be as well. As long as you are using belief and as long as you believe in caring as the source for getting people to care for themselves, you are divorcing you.

RR:

I can feel my body saying, "Oh, that's so much easier."

Gary:

Yes, you have had the experience of caring for somebody and realizing, "Oh that was so much work." I cared for my kids, but I had to let them go. I had to stop caring and be in allowance of their choices. And when I became in allowance of their choices, for the most part, they became more of who they were.

RR:

I know that works. My niece was on drugs, and I tried everything to get her to stop, and as soon as I gave it up and stopped trying to chase her around town, give her money, and sort her out, she went the right way.

Gary:

If you are trying to save people, they have to work against you. If you are trying to care for people, they have to work against you.

What have you made so vital about possessing total caring, total saving, and total believing that eliminates allowance as a factor of your reality? Everything that is times a godzillion, will you destroy and uncreate it all? Right and Wrong, Good and Bad, POD and POC, All 9, Shorts, Boys, and Beyonds.

*If you are going to have true caring,
you've got to have total allowance.*

HB:

There's a process you gave me a couple of weeks ago about "What have I made vital about the secret, hidden insanity and sickness that eliminates the very best of me?" I get that a lot of these cuckoo choices are the secret, hidden sicknesses and insanities.

Gary:

What have you made so vital about possessing the secret, hidden sicknesses and insanities that eliminate the very best of you at all times? Everything that is times a godzillion, will you destroy and uncreate it all? Right and Wrong, Good and Bad, POD and POC, All 9, Shorts, Boys, and Beyonds.

PR:

This is brilliant, thank you. There is so much freedom being created by everything we are talking about.

Gary:

As long as you are trying to believe in someone or save them, you are making the lies and the judgments greater than you. You are trying to make these people valuable and necessary to you rather than seeing that having them in your life is a choice. It's as if you think not having that choice would create something greater.

PR:

So when you have that freedom for you, it allows other people to create something greater for them ... if they choose.

Gary:

Yes. I even do this with my furniture. I ask it, "Do you want to stay or do you want to go to somebody else?" When it decides it wants to live with somebody else, someone always walks in the door and says "I love that piece! If you ever want to sell it, let me know."

I say, "You want to buy it? Here's how much it is."

They say, "Really, I can have it for that?"

I say, "Yeah." Gone! I don't try to hold on to anything. You guys are trying so hard to believe in something. You are even trying to believe in Access, so it becomes something that sucks the life out of you.

Anything you have done to believe in anything other than you, will you destroy and uncreate all that? Right and Wrong, Good and Bad, POD and POC, All 9, Shorts, Boys, and Beyonds.

CREATING VALUE WITH BELIEF

HB:

The belief I have about my birth father is a sense of "If I don't believe in him, then he has no value." I see that I am trying to create value with my belief. The sense is that if I don't do that, there's a big gaping hole in me.

Gary:

Yes, it's called "I'm not loved." But is that really a hole? Or is that a space you can walk into and have more of you?

HB:

It is that. Holy shit! And then I become my own father. I become all of those energies. I can generate them.

Gary:

You become the generative source in your life.

HB:

Yes! Rather than making other people the source of my life. Thank you! You just broke through. Thank you!

CL:

Thank you for this conversation. I have so much space and peace and joy in my body. I think a piece of it is realizing that I *be* this space with my dad—the caring, gratitude, and total allowance even though by this reality, he is a terrible father.

Gary:

By this reality, he is a nut job. He is just plain-ass nuts. Looney bins. This is a guy who was homeless on the street, telling you how to live your life.

CL:

My level of caring and allowance for him is unlike my caring for anyone on the planet.

Gary:

That is called generosity of spirit, in case you didn't know.

CL:

Cool. Well, I am sitting here asking myself what it would take to be that with everyone in my life. Because I am really clear on that energy with him and it creates so much for me. I would like more of that.

Gary:

It is total allowance and total awareness of who the person is and what they are choosing. They are choosing something that you wouldn't choose for them, but they are choosing it. It is their choice. That's just the way it is.

CL:

I adore him and he can go away if he wants.

KC:

Thank you, everyone, for this conversation about caring and allowance.

True caring is total allowance.
If you have total allowance, then whatever somebody chooses is what they choose, and you have no point of view about it.

Moving beyond Belief into Phenomenance

GET OVER THE BELIEF THAT YOU CAN CHOOSE FOR SOMEONE ELSE

KC:

During our conversation about caring, I realized that I had defined *care* as choosing better for someone. I was wondering why my ex was getting so irritated with me for caring for him. I see now that I was unknowingly projecting into his universe the wrongness of his choice to create cancer, death, and dying. He went to the rightness of suffering for his choice and I went to the rightness of choosing a greater possibility for him.

Gary:

That is the belief that you can choose for someone. You have chosen to have a greater possibility for you, and you assume that he should choose what you are choosing because you are smarter than he is. All of you have the belief that you can choose for somebody else. You have to stop believing in your choice. You decide you want to create something and you say, "Okay, I can do this." And then you define that as belief. Even if you knew what would be better for someone else, they would not be willing to choose it. You cannot choose for anyone.

Get over the belief that caring will make people better. People will be what they will be. You are not responsible for the choices they make. You're in a belief system when you believe you can get the perfect process that will make people choose better. You're in a belief system when you believe that if you had just done something right, other people wouldn't have chosen what they chose.

My basic point of view is that everything I believed was real and true has turned out to be either a lie or an implant. So what do I believe in? Nothing. What am I willing to look at? Everything. What choices do I have? All.

BELIEVING IN THE FANTASY

Disney did belief big time. He created a whole industry based on belief. As little girls, you go to bed believing that your prince will come. He will—and you'll get pregnant. And the glass slipper won't fit. You have to give up belief as a reality and start looking at what is real. You have to ask: "What's real here?" I gave up belief because everything that I had believed in turned out not to work. So I became a pragmatist. I started looking at what *would* work.

CW:

It is interesting, because when you are growing up, you are told to believe in Christmas, you are told to believe in Easter...

Gary:

And Santa Claus and the Easter Bunny and all that.

CW:

Yeah, and the "perfect" man.

Gary:

How many of you still believe there must be a perfect man or a perfect woman out there for you?

CW:

Can you say more about believing in fantasy?

Gary:

You have such an intense belief that you will find somebody, get married, and live happily ever after that you would destroy you to keep that illusion in place. How is that working for you?

CW:

It's not.

Gary:

How many Disney beliefs do you have? You've got Cinderella, Sleeping Beauty, Rapunzel, the Little Mermaid, Snow White, and you know them all.

CW:

I do.

Gary:

What have you made so vital about believing in your beliefs of love, honor, and cherish that you would destroy you to keep them?

Everything that is times a godzillion, will you destroy and uncreate it all? Right and Wrong, Good and Bad, POD and POC, All 9, Shorts, Boys, and Beyonds.

Your point of view is: "I will cease to exist if I don't have this belief to hold onto." It's your only reason for living at the moment. Is that really a good enough reason to live?

CW:

Is that why all of this sadness and depression are coming up lately?

Gary:

You are trying to believe in something you don't actually believe in. Have you found a prince anywhere? No, but you've found a lot of frogs. And no matter how many times you kissed their asses, they didn't turn into princes. What if you stopped believing in the frog that will turn into a prince and started believing in you? You've got to let go of illusions!

How many beliefs do you have to maintain to create the illusion of what should be that can never exist? Everything that is times a godzillion, will you destroy and uncreate it all? Right and Wrong, Good and Bad, POD and POC, All 9, Shorts, Boys, and Beyonds.

BELIEF OR AWARENESS?

We use belief instead of awareness. Every time you are trying to use belief in something, you are trying to cut off awareness. This is where you have to practice. You have to ask: "Am I doing belief or am I doing awareness?" "Oh, belief! How cool is that? I believe! I believe! Hallelujah, I believe!" Make fun of yourself a little bit. Play with it.

What do I believe in? Nothing.
What am I willing to look at? Everything.
What choices do I have? All.

KC:

I have so much gratitude for this conversation, because as people are speaking, I am changing.

Gary:

Do you mean that your awareness can change things? That's the great gift that I find in these conversations. In these seven-day events, people begin to realize, "Wow, everything I thought was real is not."

WT:

In the last five minutes, I finally got what belief is about. When you believe something, it stops all of the other options. It stops all of the *possibilities*.

Gary:

Yes, belief is always something that stops; it doesn't create. The majority of people in the world look for what they can believe in. There are a lot of people who come and do Access and then they leave and do something else, because they want to have beliefs. I will not provide you with beliefs. I will provide you with choices and possibilities, but not beliefs. I don't want you to believe in me. I don't want you to believe in Access, I want you *to be aware of you.* That is a very different point of view.

MN:

Is that usually why people create businesses? To believe in something? To create it as the source for their life?

Gary:

Yes, people create a business to create the source of their life instead of having fun doing something that creates money. A lot of people have the idea that if they believe firmly enough that their business is going to create, it will create. But *you*, not *your beliefs*, are the source of creation. People have all kinds of beliefs, opinions, conclusions, and other forms of judgment about business. They would have you believe that if you advertise, you will get clients. They would have you believe in doing things to get what you want rather than asking: "What am I capable of creating that would create what I want even without advertising?"

MN:

That's energetic creation.

Gary:

Yes, and energy creates way more than adverts do.

CW:

Is there something around belief with pitching something to the media?

Gary:

Yeah, how many thousands of beliefs do you have about the right way to pitch something to the media?

CW:

A lot.

Gary:

Yeah, more than a lot. So how many times have you pitched Access from some strange, off-the-wall point of view and it worked?

CW:

A lot.

Gary:

CW tries to get us on television and in the media and she always manages to pick just the right moment. And then she assumes she hasn't done enough.

CW:

What is that?

Gary:

A belief in hard work.

How many of you have dedicated your life to the belief in hard work and the idea that hard work will get you ahead? Everything that is times a godzillion, will you

destroy and uncreate it all? Right and Wrong, Good and Bad, POD and POC, All 9, Shorts, Boys, and Beyonds.

When you are creating from possibility, all things can open up and increase. If you try to create from completion or "I believe I can do this" or "I believe in myself," you aren't creating from possibility; you're trying to create from belief. How many times have you said, "I believe in myself," when it was actually a lie? Don't believe in you. *Enjoy* you. When you have the joy of being you, everything starts to work.

Belief is always something that stops; it doesn't create.

KS:

This conversation has really opened my awareness. I see how my beliefs about what I can't do are stopping the creation and the possibilities. We suck the energy out of the creation by functioning from beliefs.

Gary:

How many beliefs do you have that you can't do something? How much of your life is dedicated to beliefs of what you can't do or be rather than what you can do or be? A lot, a little or megatons? Everything that is times a godzillion, will you destroy and uncreate it all? Right and Wrong, Good and Bad, POD and POC, All 9, Shorts, Boys, and Beyonds.

What have you made so vital about possessing the purity and rightness of your beliefs that keeps you from the choice of a different possibility? Everything that is times a godzillion, will you destroy and uncreate it all? Right and

Wrong, Good and Bad, POD and POC, All 9, Shorts, Boys, and Beyonds.

KS:

If we look at creation from beyond belief, what would that look like? What would that be?

Gary:

Beyond the beliefs and the structures of the language of this reality.

How many of you have beliefs in the structure of the language of this reality? Everything that is times a godzillion, will you destroy and uncreate it all? Right and Wrong, Good and Bad, POD and POC, All 9, Shorts, Boys, and Beyonds.

It basically has to do with how you choose, because choice creates possibilities. Everything I do, whether it has to do with Access or horses or antiques, is based on a choice. I ask: "What do I need to do?" and that energy leads me in the direction I go, even if it makes absolutely no sense to me. Lots of people think I am completely insane. Lots of people think my business can't actually work, but it has been working for twenty-six years and it's getting better. So how am I wrong? I am wrong by this reality.

What have you made so vital about defining your reality by this reality that keeps you from choosing beyond this reality? Everything that is times a godzillion, will you destroy and uncreate it all? Right and Wrong, Good and Bad, POD and POC, All 9, Shorts, Boys, and Beyonds.

KS:

I am really excited about this idea of beyond belief. The few people on the planet who are creating from beyond belief don't walk around *believing* they can do it. They walk around knowing that they can do it. Is that correct?

Gary:

No, they walk around never doubting that they can choose it.

KS:

What's the difference?

Gary:

You would rather doubt your choice than choose your choice and find out where it leads you.

KS:

Yeah, that's me. That's why I am excited!

Gary:

I look at everything and I say, "I have some choices. What would I like to choose?" I never say, "I have to know what I am doing." The belief of this reality is that if you don't know exactly what you are doing and why you are doing it, the linear part of it, then you are not functioning appropriately.

AK:

We are socially inappropriate.

Gary:

The ultimate in perversion is not functioning from this reality. You guys are a bunch of perverts.

"I have some choices. What would I like to choose?"

DOUBT

KS:

You said that I would rather doubt my choice than choose my choice and find out where it leads me. Can you speak some more about that?

Gary:

Why do you doubt you?

KS:

I do not have a good answer for that. I just do it.

Gary:

Somebody just said that it keeps you entertained.

KS:

In some sense, it does keep me entertained. It also keeps me busy.

Gary:

If you were actually creating beyond this reality, entertaining yourself with this reality would never be desirable.

KS:

I get that.

Gary:

Everyone who has made it desirable to maintain their connection with this reality, their reality within this reality, and the truth of this reality being greater than their possibility, will you destroy and uncreate it all? Right and Wrong, Good and Bad, POD and POC, All 9, Shorts, Boys, and Beyonds.

KS:

So doubt is keeping the connection to this reality?

Gary:

Yes. Let me give you an example. Let's say you doubt that you are making enough money. What are you going to create? Not enough money. If you doubt you are creating enough money, you are going to create not enough money in order to make the point of view you have taken right.

How many beliefs do you have in creating from point of view as the reality of you? Everything that is times a godzillion, will you destroy and uncreate it all? Right and Wrong, Good and Bad, POD and POC, All 9, Shorts, Boys, and Beyonds.

People have this weird idea that their point of view equals who they are. Your point of view does not equal anything other than the limitations you will allow to show up in the world as you.

BELIEF AND POINT OF VIEW

LD:

What is the difference between belief and point of view?

Gary:

Unfortunately you have turned your points of view into beliefs in order to make them more substantial. A point of view is so much sexier than a belief. You try to force creation by taking a point of view and turning it into a belief. You think, "The harder I believe, the better it will get."

The Alexandria Quartet by Lawrence Durrell is four books written from four different people's points of view about the same events during the same period of time, Alexandria in the 1920s. All of these people have different points of view and their different points of view create their reality. When I read them, I was stunned to see that's the way people create, but most people try not to know that's the way they create.

What belief have you chosen to make sure you're not aware of how people create? Everything that is times a godzillion, will you destroy and uncreate it all? Right and Wrong, Good and Bad, POD and POC, All 9, Shorts, Boys, and Beyonds.

KS:

I now get your question, "Why do you doubt yourself?" I do it to stay connected to this reality.

Gary:

No, actually it's to make sure you never get out of this reality. And as long as you are never going to get out of this reality, you get to come back in and reincarnate. So, there's the next generation of you.

KS:

What else is possible with not keeping me in this reality?

Gary:

Well, do you believe in reincarnation? Or do you try not to believe in reincarnation?

KS:

Probably that.

Gary:

Whether you try not to believe in it or you try to believe in it, either one requires you to come back and do it again.

KS:

Back to the beliefs again.

Gary:

Yes, we are back to belief. Believing and not believing are two sides of the same coin. Have you ever noticed people saying, "I don't believe in that"? And how much energy do they have on saying, "I don't believe"? How much of that energy solidifies their point of view into existence? If you truly function from interesting point of view, everything that occurs would be sliding into things instead of having to push into things.

KS:

My target is to function beyond belief.

Gary:

What if you went into phenomenance instead of going beyond belief? That would be even greater, because beyond belief is only the place where you have to tap into your beliefs to determine how you can have something beyond them. And it proves that your belief is real.

KS:

I love this whole thing. I am so aware of how I have stuck myself in so many different ways with my beliefs.

Gary:

And how many lifetimes have you tried to come up with a right belief? And all of the right beliefs you have about how you should believe and how you can believe in yourself because you finally realized that what you believe about you has to be true because you've decided it is so? Everything that is times a godzillion, will you destroy and uncreate it all? Right and Wrong, Good and Bad, POD and POC, All 9, Shorts, Boys, and Beyonds.

ND:

Is being in phenomenance the total absence of point of view or belief?

Gary:

Phenomenance is not the absence of anything. It's the *inclusion* of everything.

*What if you went into phenomenance
instead of going beyond belief?*

CULTURE AND FAMILY, BELIEF AND BELONGING

BN:

You said it took courage to come here for this seven-day event. It doesn't feel like courage to me because I chose to come out of a very personal choice. It was not for anybody else; it was only for me.

Gary:

Yes, but it takes courage to do something for you. You're Indian. You are never supposed to do anything for you. Does it take courage to go against your culture and your family?

BN:

Yes.

Gary:

Here's the thing: You're an infinite being. You're not your culture. You're not your family. You're not any of that. Are you an Indian? No, you're an infinite being.

What have you made so vital about never possessing the totality of the phenomenance of infinite being that keeps you choosing to believe the stupids in your reality? Everything that is times a godzillion, will you destroy and uncreate it all? Right and Wrong, Good and Bad, POD and POC, All 9, Shorts, Boys, and Beyonds.

Apparently a lot of you love believing in stupids. "I believe in idiots."

What have you made so vital about never possessing the total capacity of infinite being, the phenomenance of infinite being, that keeps you believing in the stupids around you? Everything that is times a godzillion, will you destroy and uncreate it all? Right and Wrong, Good and Bad, POD and POC, All 9, Shorts, Boys, and Beyonds.

BN:

When you were talking about that, a couple of things came up for me. The word *belonging* comes up. And *belief.*

Gary:

Belief and belonging. How many of you believe your family loves you? Get over it. Everything that is times a godzillion, will you destroy and uncreate it all? Right and Wrong, Good and Bad, POD and POC, All 9, Shorts, Boys, and Beyonds.

How many of you know you love your family better than they love themselves? That doesn't mean you have to believe in them, that doesn't mean you have to love them, that just means you have to recognize, "Okay, I love them better than they love themselves." Be aware. Don't make yourself the victim of your family. Everything that is times a godzillion, will you destroy and uncreate it all? Right and Wrong, Good and Bad, POD and POC, All 9, Shorts, Boys, and Beyonds.

BN:

You have said, "Don't make peace; make waves."

Gary:

Yes, don't make peace; make waves. You should know how to make waves. You've been making waves with your family forever, haven't you? Haven't you always been the black sheep of the family?

BN:

Yes.

Gary:

Haven't you always been the one who stirred the pot when everybody else was making peace? Haven't they told you that you need to settle down and not be so weird?

BN:

Yes.

Gary:

I took that out of your head. So, what's the truth? Do you love your family more than they love you?

BN:

Yes.

Gary:

Do you believe in your culture?

BN:

Ummm, not as much.

Gary:

That would be a *yes*.

BN:

That's where the belonging comes in.

Gary:

I understand that. Aren't we clever? We believe in our culture when it's not working for us. We believe in our family when they don't like us. We believe in the best in people when all we see is the worst. We believe in being idiots and stupids.

Everywhere you have decided you need to believe so you can be an idiot or a stupid, will you destroy and uncreate all that? Right and Wrong, Good and Bad, POD and POC, All 9, Shorts, Boys, and Beyonds.

What greater possibility are you refusing that you truly could be choosing, that if you would choose it, would give you the ability to be the gift you truly be? Everything that is times a godzillion, will you destroy and uncreate it all? Right and Wrong, Good and Bad, POD and POC, All 9, Shorts, Boys, and Beyonds.

The blessing of possibility is that you begin to realize that nothing is more real than you make it. Why do you make things real that are not?

AK:

To have some kind of reference point.

Gary:

It's a reference for being what other people want you to be. What if you never had to be what other people wanted you to be? What if you only got to be what *you* wanted to be? It's called creating your own reality.

What have you made so vital about never possessing the awareness of your reality that keeps you living by the gift and limitation of other people's insanity? Everything that is times a godzillion, will you destroy and uncreate it all? Right and Wrong, Good and Bad, POD and POC, All 9, Shorts, Boys, and Beyonds.

The blessing of possibility is that you begin to realize

that nothing is more real than you make it.

BN:

I have been looking at what made me choose the family I have.

Gary:

You knew they wouldn't be able to control you. They tried. How did that work? Can anybody control you? Truth? You're so cute. You're trying to lie and say *yes*. You know it is a lie.

BN:

Am I controlling me with the illusion that they are controlling me?

Gary:

Yes. It is much more fun to blame them than to say you are doing it, isn't it? It is such a gift to be able to blame everything on your parents. "They screwed me up, they screwed me up, they screwed me up. They are always trying to control me, so I have to fight them." No, you fight because it is fun for you. If you were a man child, you would be a Sumo wrestler.

What if you never had to be what other people wanted you to be?
What if you only got to be what you wanted to be? It's called creating your own reality.

LD:

You routinely tease me about having been a Mormon. Do I still have a lot of that holding me back?

Gary:

You like your family.

LD:

I do like my family.

Gary:

Yes, you have it holding you back. When you like your family, you don't want to disappoint them nor do you want to offend them. So you will shut of parts of you to make sure you don't offend. You won't be everything you are because it might be offensive. Now, it is not bad to do that if you know you are doing it.

LD:

I think I am getting better at that. My sister is helping me with my work, and she is not too scared of what I'm doing in Access. That's pretty exciting.

Gary:

She's not too scared; she's only slightly scared.

LD:

She tells me that my brothers don't know what I'm doing, and I say, "I know." She says, "Well, they have to know," and I say, "No, they don't. They don't have to understand what I do." What else could I be or do?

Gary:

You could say, "I get that, but I know that what I am doing would be difficult for them, so I would rather they didn't know." Then it is all about them.

I was married to my second wife for sixteen years. The last year we were together her mother had congestive heart failure and came to stay with us for six weeks. As she walked out of the room on the last night she was at our house, she said, "You know what? I realize I know nothing about your life. We must chat some time. Goodnight." Sixteen years and she never asked me a single question. I didn't try to keep the peace; I just didn't create waves. Are you trying to create peace? When you are creating peace, you are eliminating you. When you are not making waves unless it works for you, you have a different reality.

LD:

I realized recently that one of the greatest gifts my mother gave me was dying. She set me free.

Gary:

It was a gift because it required you to choose not for her but for you.

LD:

We had a great relationship, but she knew that for me to go to the next step, I had to…

Gary:

She was not your normal Mormon woman, and she knew that if you were going to choose to be the not-normal Mormon in your family, the only way you could do it is if she got out of the way.

LD:

Yes, because everybody in the family has always told me that everything strange I ever did was her fault. It was never me. It was all her fault.

Gary:

She was about four feet tall and weighed nothing, but they blamed everything on her. Nice family. I love families—*not.*

TS:

The family thing. I love those idiots. It is like AA. "I am TS and I love my parents." I am now spending more time in the city where my parents are. They live five minutes from me. They would love to have me to sit in their laps.

Gary:

You are the baby. What don't you get? They didn't realize that you were going to turn out to be a babe. They thought you were always going to be a baby.

TS:

What you just talked about with LD brought up some interesting awareness about my choices. What else is possible?

Gary:

Invite your parents over for dinner. Have a really cute guy there. Say to your parents, "I want you to meet my insignificant other," and then talk to them all night long and ask them questions about themselves. Tell them nothing about you.

TS:

Cook dinner for my parents, invite some cute guy over, and then ask them questions about them? What will that create?

Gary:

They'll think you are going down a normal road.

SM:

I did that at Christmas. I invited a guy, somebody I sleep with, to come over for Christmas dinner and my mother immediately assumed that he is my future something. I told her, "He's great! He's a waiter." She stopped asking questions because he didn't fit her profile of my dedicated husband.

You should have seen her face. And now she doesn't ask any questions about that part of my life.

My dad had a conversation with me when my mom wasn't there. He said, "Honey, I don't care if you choose a waiter or if you never produce a grandchild. I just want you to know that I don't have a point of view about this."

Gary:

Your dad is cool.

TS:

Yes, he is. He would be happy if I got married, but he really doesn't have a point of view about it. The waiter thing was pretty funny.

Gary:

That was brilliant.

TS:

It wasn't too cruel?

Gary:

No, it just played into her prejudices. Always play into somebody's weak point and then you control the card game. You just introduced two jokers with that guy.

HB:

Is all that true?

TS:

Oh, yes, very true!

When you are creating peace, you are eliminating you.
When you are not making waves unless it works for you,
you have a different reality.

DO YOU BELIEVE IN FAMILY?

NK:

When you were talking to LD about her family, I was thinking, "Why would anyone choose to be around that?" yet I know I am doing the same thing. What would it take for me to see more clearly where my family is functioning from?

Gary:

Do you believe in family?

NK:

I still do, yes.

Gary:

How many beliefs are you believing that allow them to punish you continuously?

NK:

A hell of a lot.

Gary:

Why would you rather be punished than have your reality?

NK:

It's like I deserve it or it's normal.

Gary:

It ain't because you deserve it. It's more like "I'm so tough, I can take it. They can beat me, but I won't cry. They can take advantage of me, use me, and not pay me anything. I'll just take it."

NK:

That's pretty much where I am now. What's it going to take to move beyond that? I am ready to totally give them up.

Gary:

No, you're not. You lie.

What have you made so vital about never possessing the phenomenance of total consciousness that keeps you from living the limited life you currently live?

Everything that is times a godzillion, will you destroy and uncreate it all? Right and Wrong, Good and Bad, POD and POC, All 9, Shorts, Boys, and Beyonds.

When you like your family, you don't want to disappoint them, nor do you want to offend them.
So you will shut off parts of you to
make sure you don't offend.

THE PHENOMENANCE OF PARENTING

KT:

I've been constantly fighting with my teenage son. Recently I got to the space with him where I knew I had to do something totally different. I said to him, "Okay, you have choice now. You can do whatever you want."

He asked, "What do you mean?"

I said, "You have choice. You can choose to do whatever you want. Just remember that I have choice too. Choice creates awareness."

He asked, "What do you mean?"

I said, "You'll find out."

For a few weeks he was off doing whatever he was doing. Then one day a parent came to the front door with her drunken son and my drunken son. She said they had stolen her bottle of Cointreau and were having shots.

I said, "Okay, you've done it this time. I'm stepping back in now."

He said, "Why weren't you telling me off last week or the week before? Why did you let me do it?" He thinks I am stupid and I don't know what he's up to.

Gary:

You might have said, "Son, I knew what you were doing. As long as you kept it off of other parents' lines, I didn't care. But now you have put me in a position where they could take you away and put you in foster care. I wasn't sure I was willing to have that but I might reconsider it and suggest foster care, anyway. Or you can go back and live with your dad."

KT:

I have suggested that. His manipulation is "If you do that, I am going to run away."

Gary:

Then you could say, "Okay, that's a choice. The nice thing about runaway kids is they usually become prostitutes and I think you would probably be good at that."

KT:

That's not a visual I…

Gary:

Oh, that's not a visual you want to give your kid? You are not willing to be mean enough to make him take care of himself? Look at it. What's going to make him choose something different? You could try, "Yeah, running away is a good idea because most runaways become prostitutes and I'm sure a lot of old men would love your ass."

KT:

I can just see his reaction. That would be funny.

Gary:

You've got to use all of your weapons. You've got to be smarter than the little shit. The phenomenance of parenting is always being willing to let your children choose and not have a point of view.

The phenomenance of parenting is always being willing to let your children choose and not have a point of view.

Rejection and Receiving

Gary:

I have been having conversations with a couple of people and I asked MN, in particular, to share her point of view with you. She told me she doesn't have a reference point for where she is, because from her point of view, it is normal to be sliced, diced, and rejected. She was looking at the friendships she had before she came to Access, and she saw that those friends were using her. As soon as she went to Access and started creating her own life that wasn't revolving around theirs, they dumped her. This is where a lot of you have sat. If what you do doesn't revolve around the people in your life, they reject you. Then you assume there is something wrong with you.

BEING REJECTED AND DISCARDED

When I was a kid I had two best friends. I introduced them to each other. I thought the three of us could have a great time together, but they rejected and excluded me. They were really mean to me. I said, "Wow, that is so unkind. I will never do that to anybody." So I have never been willing to discard anybody. I will let people reject me and go away if they choose, but I will never discard them.

Those of you who were rejected at one time or another would never reject someone else because you have felt the pain of it. You have felt the insanity of it. You have said, "I won't do that to anybody." Others doing it to you seems normal, but you doing it to them seems impossible. When do you get to receive?

MN:

You don't get to receive. The thing I saw this morning was that every time someone says, "You look beautiful" or "I love you," or every time someone wants to hug me, I so badly want to push that away or reject it. You asked me if I like me.

Gary:

How about the rest of you? Do you like you?

PN:

Occasionally.

Gary:

Occasionally, yeah. That's the place where others rejected you and where you rejected you. To have your reality, you've got to realize what you like about you. Play with what you like about you. *Please.* Because until you can receive you, you can't assume anything, except that you will be rejected.

Your reality has been "I will not reject but I will be rejected." If you function from "I will be rejected, I will be left out" as your primary point of view, you are always prepared for that and you can deal with it, because you've dealt with it your whole life.

MN:

It seems crazy to me that I would choose to be discarded in such an ugly way for my whole life.

Gary:

It was easier for you to do that than to receive people who cared for you. The problem you are having with RD right now is that he cares too much and that's scary for you because you don't have defense systems and automatic reject systems in place. You have to choose what's a reality for you. You have to say, "You know what? I really like this person being present with me."

MN:

Or I don't like it. I honestly have no idea how I feel about anybody at the moment.

Gary:

That's the thing of getting clear about what your reality is. That is where you have to start functioning from the question. You have to practice and play at creating. You have to ask: "If I were creating my reality today, what would I choose? Would I choose to reject RD or would I choose to care for him?" And since you are prepared for rejection, you will never let yourself feel, perceive, and receive the level of caring that is actually you.

MN:

I can care for him and I can care for others. It is *their* caring for me that I judge.

Gary:

That's what you can't receive. When you are a person who has been discarded or rejected, you expect more rejection. From your perspective, rejection is totally normal. That's what you have received your entire life. To not be rejected is totally unfamiliar and weird to you. You have to see what your reality is and ask, "Okay so what could I create that I have never considered?"

MN:

It makes me want to throw up.

Gary:

I know. I have had five people tell me, "I want to throw up. What's wrong with me?" *Nothing* is wrong with you. Something is changing, and it disorients you. In the past, balance was created based on all the things you experienced as a kid, all the rejections and discardments you had. Now something is changing.

MN:

Honestly, I have no idea who I am or how I will be. Previously I've always liked to have my ducks in a row. I wanted to have a level of control. I now see that that is based on rejection.

Gary:

You would have your ducks in a row so no matter how somebody discarded you, you would know where you were. Do any of the rest of you recognize this?

Anything you have done to make being discarded your balance point in life, will you destroy and uncreate it all? Right and Wrong, Good and Bad, POD and POC, All 9, Shorts, Boys, and Beyonds.

What balance point have you chosen that is sliding out of existence as we speak? Everything that is times a godzillion, will you destroy and uncreate it all? Right and Wrong, Good and Bad, POD and POC, All 9, Shorts, Boys, and Beyonds.

When you get to this raw place, it is three days to suffer and then you will have a new space, a new possibility, a new level of awareness, and a new level of receiving that will shock you in its ease.

MN:

I get that. When I was out walking today, I was saying, "I know I will come out the other side" because that's what I do.

Gary:

You always do.

> *Since you are prepared for rejection, you will*
> *never let yourself feel, perceive, and receive*
> *the level of caring that is actually you.*

REJECT BEFORE YOU GET REJECTED

MA:

Since I have been doing Access, I have more and more people who care about me and have my back, but I notice I have a tendency to go to "How can I separate from them before they reject me?"

Gary:

You have created "Reject before you get rejected" as your reality. Do you want to continue that reality?

MA:

No.

Gary:

Then you have to ask: "What can I choose different that would work better for me?" You have to choose to have no judgment, because it is primarily your judgment of you that gets you to separate from others.

MA:

I watch my students do this, and I would like to inspire something else.

Gary:

The only way you are going to inspire that is if you are being something else. You have to choose to be something different.

> *It is primarily your judgment of you that gets you to separate from others.*

DISMISSAL

CL:

My question is about dismissal. Is that similar to discarding? A few years ago a group of us were at a restaurant, and the waiter told me they didn't have something I wanted. I reacted in a certain way, and you asked me, "Why did you just dismiss the waiter?" I see that this is an energy I choose sometimes.

Gary:

It is similar to discarding, but it is done from a place of superiority. You probably learned it from your hippie parents.

CL:

Superiority?

Gary:

They were superior in their poverty. Rather than saying, "This is our lifestyle. You can like it or not," they would dismiss people on the basis that they didn't understand the brilliance of their lifestyle. Dismissal then became a way of rejecting from a position of "I've got to be better than they are because these people don't get how good I am," which means they had to be in judgment of whom?

CL:

Themselves.

Gary:

Yes.

CL:

I would like to change that energy. It is not the first thing I function from, but I go to it when something…

Gary:

What part of that is vital to your reality?

CL:

It has something to do with survival.

Gary:

Isn't that what your parents tried to teach you to do? Survive without anything?

CL:

Yeah.

Gary:

And then dismiss anybody who wasn't as smart as they were for surviving without. That's judgment. As a kid, you learned the judgment of the rightness of your point of view.

CL:

Yes.

Gary:

Which is in absolute opposition to your basic generosity of spirit.

CL:

I can only hear about every three words you are saying. It's like last year when we got to my need to be right. It felt like the one thing that I couldn't overcome.

Gary:

Yes, because it is such a foundation of your reality.

CL:

Yet it's in total opposition to my being.

Gary:

You're not seeing how these things fit together. I looked at this stuff and I asked, "How do these things fit together?" I can't do judgment; therefore, I can't dismiss because dismissal is based on judgment; therefore, I have to be right in order to have a judgment.

CL:

When I look at it, I don't get that judgment is part of my reality at all.

Gary:

No, but rightness is part of your reality. When you need to be right, you're always waiting for someone to be wrong so you can leave.

CL:

How can judgment not be part of my reality but rightness is?

Gary:

Because you make rightness part of your point of view and you assume that's not judgment.

CL:

So I have excluded rightness from judgment?

Gary:

Yeah.

CL:

It's not judgment if I am right. I get it.

Gary:

Exactly. Now you are getting it. You get the point of view "I must be right; *therefore*...." As long as there is a *therefore*, you think it is not a judgment. It's a given. The therefore is the given. It's the way it is. "I'm right; therefore you are not right."

CL:

Even "I am not right" is a given that somehow I am right underneath not being right.

Gary:

No matter which way you go, "I'm right."

CL:

It's not my fault I'm not right.

Gary:

That's where you make it part of your reality to be right. I never have the point of view that I have to be right or that I am right, which is why I can change a point of view. You saw how getting that different point of view with HB flipped my whole world. HB showed me a place where I had assumed a point of view about the way everybody else would see the world, which actually wasn't true. I realized I had created a narrow band based on a point of view that I thought everybody else had.

My point of view was that it was a gift to me when people showed me what they were actually doing or when they rejected me. HB didn't have the point of view that it was a gift, and when she said that, I said, "Oh my God! I've been trying to get people to see the gift it is when people expose themselves in that way, and that is *not* where other people live." I had assumed they did.

When you need to be right, you're always waiting
for someone to be wrong so you can leave.

YOU HAVE CREATED YOUR REALITY
AROUND THE VALUE OF JUDGMENT

HB:

You said that when you learned judgment was destructive, you stopped doing it. There is something in that that was so obvious for you. When you talk about it, I see what you're saying and I want to agree with you—but I don't truly believe it.

Gary:

Do you get that your point of view is a choice?

HB:

I absolutely get that. But do I *really* get that? I must not.

Gary:

You couldn't have the point of view that judgment is right.

HB:

I don't have the point of view that judgment is right or wrong. It's just a thing that…

Gary:

You have made vital to your reality.

HB:

The other day when I was in the lobby, you walked by, and we had a few words. As you walked away, I felt so happy. I felt this open warmth growing in my chest. I asked, "How did he do that?" Most of the time when I talk to you, there's a wonderful, easy joy that becomes available. NK described it the other day. He said, "After I talk to Gary, everything feels so easy and great."

When you said that you learned that judgment created destruction, I said, "Okay! *That's* how he is doing it." And for a second I slipped into that reality and that universe, but it is not where I tend to live from.

Gary:

It's not your reality.

HB:

What do I need to change or get?

Gary:

It is a choice. You have created your reality around the value of judgment.

HB:

Just this morning, I woke up with some big-time judgment of myself. I said to NK, "Honey, you seem so distant" and he said, "You're just judging yourself a lot right now," and I said, "Oh, right."

Gary:

Yes, he was saying, "You're judging yourself so you can be as far away from me as possible." You have to get what you have created as your reality and decide whether you want to keep that as your reality. We are having this conversation not because I am trying to get you to change. I am trying to get you to see how you are creating your reality so you can choose what you want to create as your reality instead of going back to the same old thing again and again.

HB:

I am getting a whole new perspective on this thing. You have asked so many times, "What would you like to choose to create as your reality?" I'm hearing it in a whole different way right now.

Gary:

Yes!

> *I am trying to get you to see how you are creating*
> *your reality so you can choose what you want*

to create as your reality instead of going back
to the same old thing again and again.

INCLUDING EVERYONE

FB:

I am making a demand of myself to include everyone in my life. You have told me that you have to reach for me three times before I'll respond. Is there something I need to practice to change this?

Gary:

Practice always answering phone calls, emails, and everything else as soon as they come in. I've noticed that if you are planning to go to a class or some other event, you'll respond to a text or a Skype and just end it without mentioning that you'll be going to the class. You never give people a sense of completion that allows them to know you will be there in the future.

If I send somebody an email and they respond to me, I send them a "Thanks" back. They send me a text, and oftentimes I make a one-word response. Somebody said that I was the king of the one-word response. I will always respond so people see that I am still there in some way. I have not just left them. I have not cut them off. I have not excluded them.

RR:

Most people are too busy to send all of those texts.

Gary:

No, they are not too busy. They are too separated, and they don't want to be connected to you. A while back, my kids were always saying, "You're never home! You're never home!" and then as soon as I was home, they would go to see their friends. I finally got that they didn't actually want me. They just wanted to know they could have me. So I asked, "How can I be that for them?" I realized that I could keep energy with them, and as long as I kept an energy there, they felt connected to me.

FB:

That doesn't feel as much like allowing people into my life as allowing myself out of something.

Gary:

It's allowing you into their life. If you let somebody into your life, a different possibility can occur. If you have been rejected and discarded, you tend not to let people in. It seems normal to be discarded, so you won't let people into your life, and you don't let you into their life. That way you already are discarded by the fact that you won't let you in there. What if you had as your reality "There will be no separation between me and others"? That's my point of view.

FB:

That's what I am asking for.

Gary:

You have to choose it. "My reality is there will be no separation between me and others."

FB:

The other day you told me that if I was going to include everyone, I needed to include myself...

Gary:

Because there's always a place where you withdraw so you are prepared for others to withdraw.

FB:

Yes, I have constantly anticipated judgment, rejection, or separation, even from you.

Gary:

You assume I am judging you when I am not.

FB:

I know. I also do that with MN and RD, who are some of the most wonderful friends I have ever had.

Gary:

And they do not judge you at all.

FB:

Yes.

If you let somebody into your life,
a different possibility can occur.

DISCARDMENT, REJECTION, AND RIGHTNESS

PR:

I get that discardment and rejection have been elements through my entire life. When you talked with CL about being right, I saw that was mixed in with it for me. Can you talk a little more about how to undo that?

Gary:

It's not about undoing anything; it is about recognizing "This has been part of my reality," and then asking, "Do I wish to have this as my reality any longer?" Then it's "I'm going to do or be whatever it takes for this to no longer be part of my reality." Every time it comes up you'll have to go to "Interesting point of view," because it will come back. You've had it your whole life. You've been assuming that it's the way things are and the way things are done. It doesn't have to be like that. We keep assuming that once we've seen it, we've got to find a way out of it. There is no way out of it. There's just choice for it or against it. This is where choice creates.

In the moment that it occurs, you say, "Okay, good, I'm doing anger again" or "I'm doing judgment and I would choose this for what frigging reason?" When you do anger or judgment or whatever it is, you define your reality as a finite being instead of going to the question, "Would an infinite being choose this?" And if an infinite being wouldn't choose it, why are you?

PR:

I have never been able to do "Interesting point of view" like you did.

Gary:

You have never wanted to do it because it would destroy your rightness.

PR:

Yes, that's what I am seeing today.

Gary:

And that's what a whole lot of people don't want to do—they don't want to destroy their rightness.

PR:

What creates that?

Gary:

Choice. You choose to maintain your rightness. Being right is somehow vital to your reality. And if you have been discarded or rejected in any part of your life, choosing to be right seems like your best choice. It seems that if you aren't right, you have no reality. You don't get that reality is just a creation. It's not a solidification. It can change any moment depending on what you would like to have as your reality.

PR:

Can you talk about how allowance plays into this?

Gary:

If you need to be right, you can have no allowance. If you need to be angry, you can have no allowance. If you need to judge, you can have no allowance. If you have no allowance of you, your partner seems to be distant from you. If you have no allowance of you, your partner must always be distant from you, because you have ceased to be you with him. And you always think it's his fault, by the way.

CL:

I want to add something you said to me a couple of months ago, which has been coming back in the last few days: "It is now time to choose what kind of person you would like to be." HB said that again to me the other day. That's what this is about.

Gary:

If you really want to get there, you have to say, "Judgment will never be a part of my reality again, period. I will not have judgment of me or anyone else as part of my reality." You have to make that demand of yourself for that to be your reality—or it doesn't work.

SP:

I see how much rightness is part of my reality. When you said, "You choose your point of view," I thought, "Yeah, but there are some right points of view." You just said, "I will not have judgment in my reality." Is it really that easy?

Gary:

Yes. No point of view is right. It's just your point of view.

SP:

I am becoming aware of how much I have rejected and discarded me in everything.

Gary:

Yes, in order to be right.

SP:

And then I go to conclusion to try to be right.

Gary:

Yes. The only way you can be right is if you are in conclusion.

SP:

It's that simple? Just choosing "I'll have this."

Gary:

Yeah "I'll have this. I won't have that." You have to ask: "What do I want to choose?" Not "What have I chosen?" and "How do I make what I have chosen right somehow?" You choose things. It is that simple. When you choose something, do you have to keep choosing it, or do you have a new possibility? Where do you want to live? In possibility or in conclusion? Once you go to "I am right," you are in conclusion, and no possibility that doesn't match that can ever come into your awareness—*ever.*

SP:

Which would be all of the things I haven't been able to change.

Gary:

Yeah, it is all of the things you haven't been able to change because somewhere you made some part of it right so you wouldn't have to change.

Where do you want to live? In possibility or in conclusion?

The Phenomenance
of your Reality

Gary:

When I was a kid we lived in a little house, and we had the same furniture for years. When a couch would wear out, my parents would buy a new one and put it in exactly the same place. They never rearranged the furniture. Nothing was ever different. I said, "Mom, I don't like this. I don't want to live like this. Everything is always in the same place."

She said, "Yes, that way you always know where everything is."

Do you remember melmac dishes? You couldn't break them if you tried. I tried. We had melmac dishes that were grey and pink. And aluminum glasses that were pink, blue, green, orange, and gold. You couldn't break those either.

My aunt lived in a beautiful house with beautiful furniture and Oriental rugs. Her dishes were china and her glassware was crystal. She had sterling silver flatware. I said, "When I grow up I am going to live like this! How do I get there from where I am?" That was when I began to create my reality. You've got to decide what you are going to have in your life, whatever it is, and go for it. As you go for it, greater things begin to show up.

MP:

I don't allow myself to have crystal glasses in my life because I don't want to break them. I don't want to break anything.

Gary:

You don't want to break anything, because if you break it, you will have to get something better to replace it.

MP:

I am really coming from a penurious reality.

Gary:

You are coming from a penurious reality and you are not willing to have money as a result of it.

MP:

This is not actually my reality. It's my mother's.

Gary:

Exactly. You've got to get what your reality is.

You've got to decide what you are going to have in your life, whatever it is, and go for it.
As you go for it, greater things begin to show up.

WHAT ARE YOU NOT WILLING TO GIVE UP TO HAVE YOUR REALITY?

BN:

You once asked, "What you are not willing to give up to have your reality?" I got "My mother and her family."

Gary:

You're not willing to give up your mother and her family, so you will never have your own reality. Her reality is more important than yours. It's the same for NK. You can't have *your* reality if your reality is based on someone else's needs, wants, requires, or desires.

You can have your reality and be aware of somebody's needs, requires, and desires and then do what they need, require, and desire if you want to, but you can't create your reality based on *their* needs. Most of you think that if your family needs something, you must adjust you to give them that.

I will do something if it pleases me. For example, I know what all my kids desire of me and I'll do it if I want to. If I don't want to do it, I ain't going to do it. That's a totally different reality.

What have you made so vital about never possessing the phenomenance of your reality that keeps you a slave, a servant, and a subject of this reality? That's sort of like "All hail to the queen," but who is the queen? It ain't you. Everything that is times a godzillion, will you destroy and uncreate it all? Right and Wrong, Good and Bad, POD and POC, All 9, Shorts, Boys, and Beyonds.

NC:

I have almost no communication with my family, but I am still letting them control me. I'm not operating in my own reality.

Gary:

How much of what you do is based on what they would like of you? A seventy-four-year-old lady came to a class. I said, "You've got to have this, this, and this."

She said, "My mother would never approve of that."

I said, "Your mother would never approve? You're seventy-four. How old is your mother?"

"She died."

"How long ago?"

"Twenty-eight years ago."

"Almost thirty years later, you're running your life based on what your mother would approve of? That's frigging nuts."

Do you still look to see what your family would be approving of?

You can't have your reality if your reality is based on someone else's needs, wants, requires, or desires.

"ONE DAY MY FAMILY WILL COME"

NK:

So for me, is it the beliefs and the illusions of what my family thought?

Gary:

No, it is your belief and illusion in what *you* thought your family was going to be and do.

NK:

For me?

Gary:

No, what you thought they were going to be and do, period. You are never in the computation with your family. Is that at all real to you?

NK:

Yeah, I'm getting that. I definitely see that—because they never ask questions about anything.

Gary:

They don't like you.

NK:

Where do I go with that?

Gary:

What do you mean, "Where do I go with that?"

NK:

Do I totally divorce them, cut them out of my life?

Gary:

Did I say that?

NK:

No.

Gary:

Where do you go with that? You go to "They don't really like me." Then you will stop expecting things from them that you can't get. You keep expecting them to somehow turn around. Your belief is "One day my family will come."

NK:

They will come ... and see my point of view. And see me.

Gary:

Do you think they care? They don't give a shit about your point of view. They are not interested in you unless you are a reflection of their sperm quality and egg quality. Why do you let them work you to the bone in return for a promise, a promissory note for a possibility of a future they will never deliver? What part of them do you value more than you?

NK:

Their approval still. Getting it right.

Gary:

I tell you that your family doesn't like you, and you say, "Yes, but I want their approval." You cannot get approval from somebody who doesn't like you. But you still want their approval. So you bend, fold, staple, and mutilate yourself to try and get what they will never give you. How's that working for you?

NK:

It doesn't work at all. How else can I be with my family? I have seen the approval thing for so long and I'm over that.

Gary:

No, you're not over it! You still go back to it. It is the first thing you say any time I ask you a question. You are not over it. You still desire their approval, and somewhere you actually think they are going to give it. That's the illusion you are creating. It's the same illusion CW has. "Someday someone will see who I am and appreciate me." Instead of "What the hell am I doing? How stupid can I actually be?"

NK:

You asked a question that really resonated with me: "What would I like to do that is going to create my reality today?"

Gary:

You will never create your reality unless it gets approval from your family.

NK:

That's not exactly true, because there are a lot of things I choose these days that they would not approve of.

Gary:

Do you share those things with them?

NK:

I can't share that with them. They don't care. They don't see anything.

Gary:

Are you still seeking their approval?

NK:

Will my willingness to go away from the family begin to change this?

Gary:

You've got to get what your reality is. Right now you are trying to create the place of illusion that your family will finally love you and care for you.

You haven't chosen your reality because you won't choose a reality that does not create approval from your family. Why is your family more important than you?

OTHER POSSIBILITIES EXIST FOR YOU

RJ:

I grew up with an extremely dominant father who was a street fighter and a boxer, and I got stomped on if I came up with something that was different from what my father wanted to have.

Gary:

So how much of your reality did you create from being the opposite of your dad?

RJ:

A lot.

Gary:

Is that serving you?

RJ:

No.

Gary:

How much have you tried to create who you are based on "I will never do x, y, z." But you want to be able to do x, y, z, whatever it is. Your dad abused you rather dynamically, didn't he? Because he wanted to make you tough and mean like he was.

RJ:

Exactly.

Gary:

And you refused to be tough and mean. But in not being willing to be tough and mean, you've eliminated some of your awareness, and because of that, you have been taken advantage of by people. Always be willing to be everything. That's my reality. "I am everything." I have been or done everything in one lifetime or another.

That's a different reality because it keeps you in a place where a different possibility can show up. You've got to be willing to destroy everything you created based on your dad.

Everything you defined as your reality based on being his reality and not having his reality, will you destroy and uncreate all that? Right and Wrong, Good and Bad, POD and POC, All 9, Shorts, Boys, and Beyonds.

Other possibilities exist for you. You have probably never recognized that you are much more creative than your dad was. Fighting was the only thing he had. You have more than that. And he didn't like the fact that you were smarter than he was, which is why he stomped you to death every time you came up with an idea that was more brilliant than the one he came up with.

RJ:

And also sexually. When I was fifteen or sixteen, there was a girl I was interested in. She was gorgeous, and we were playing and kissing. At a dinner party with some friends I was talking about her, and my dad got so angry that he hit me across the head and walked off. I don't know what that was.

Gary:

It was envy. Jealousy is wanting to take away what someone else has. Envy is wanting what someone has.

RJ:

I was making out with the same girl in a park a year or so later, and my brother told my mum. My mum came driving across the park in the car. She said, "Get in the car and come home." When I did, she said, "I never want you to speak to that girl or go near her again." I remember shutting down my sexualness and all of my sexual energy at that time.

Gary:

Yes, we give up so much of our sexual capacity because we assume that there is something wrong with the choices we make. There is never anything wrong.

Always be willing to be everything. That's my reality.
"I am everything." I have been or done
everything in one lifetime or another.

MAKING YOURSELF A SLAVE TO THIS REALITY

Many of you are talking about all of the things you *can't* do. I keep trying to show you that you have a reality where you *can* do. Your reality and what you are capable of are greater than what you are willing to have. You keep looking at this reality. You have made yourself a slave to this reality, so everything you look at is based on this reality.

TS:

When I ask, "What else is possible?" for creating the things I am interested in, I reference things through this reality—what it would take, how it should look, and all that crap. It keeps me in a no-choice energy.

Gary:

That is how you make yourself a slave and a servant of this reality. That is not in your best interest. You haven't been taught to choose your own reality or to create it.

What have you made so vital about never possessing the awareness of your reality that keeps you living by the gift and limitation of other people's insanity? Everything that is times a godzillion, will you destroy and uncreate it all? Right and Wrong, Good and Bad, POD and POC, All 9, Shorts, Boys, and Beyonds.

ES:

I have been putting so much energy into buying into this reality, creating this reality, and maintaining this reality.

This is the first time I've had a sense of a different choice. I am so grateful for the possibility of that.

BD:

Can you talk about seeing things through the eyes of this reality—and what else is possible?

Gary:

You have trained yourself to see through the eyes of this reality. You have never trained yourself to look at your own reality. You've got to get over training and entraining to this reality by what you *see*, and instead choose to create the possibilities by what you can *be*. You try to see everything through the eyes of this reality, the eyes of judgment, and the places other people function from. What if you could be something that was so different that nobody would ever be able to control you again?

What have you made so vital about never possessing the phenomenance of your reality that keeps you from choosing beyond this one? Everything that is times a godzillion, will you destroy and uncreate it all? Right and Wrong, Good and Bad, POD and POC, All 9, Shorts, Boys, and Beyonds.

BD:

I am having glimpses of that. I will have the instantaneous awareness of what my reality is. I won't be looking to see things through the eyes of this reality, and then something occurs and this reality is all I see.

Gary:

That is not an occurrence; it's a creation. Nothing *occurs* in your life. You *create* it. You are creating that for what reason? When you call something an occurrence, you are not acknowledging the fact that you are creating it, that you are choosing it, and that it is something that has some value to you. You don't ask:

+ I would think this has value based on what?
+ An infinite being would choose this for what reason?

What have you made so valuable about never possessing the phenomenance of your reality that keeps you functioning as a subject and slave to this reality? Do any of you get that you have been a slave to this reality? Has it been fun? "Yes, I love being a slave. I get no food. I get nothing. I get whipped and beaten by everybody around me so I know I have value." What? If you are a slave, you have value, don't you? They won't let you go because they don't want to lose the control they have over you. They like that. It makes them happy. The only way you have value is by being a slave to this reality. This is the primary source for the creation of what you have decided is your value being enslaved by this reality—or by someone in this reality.

Everything that is times a godzillion, will you destroy and uncreate it all? Right and Wrong, Good and Bad, POD and POC, All 9, Shorts, Boys, and Beyonds.

> *Your reality and what you are capable of are*
> *greater than what you are willing to have.*

COMFORT AND DISCOMFORT

MT:

I have been playing with being uncomfortable. My ease with it has increased but...

Gary:

You have decided what *uncomfortable* is. You say, "This is uncomfortable. It feels like shit." What you *don't* do—and what you *need to do*—is ask:

+ What is this?
+ What can I do with it?
+ Can I change it?
+ If so, how do I change it?

What if everything you have been asking for requires you to exist in this space of *not comfortable?*

What if *uncomfortable* is an indication that you are getting everything you would actually like to have and *comfortable* means you get to be like everybody else?

You have made *uncomfortable* wrong, wrong, so very wrong. "It is wrong to be uncomfortable. *Uncomfortable* means some wrongness is about to occur." But the only thing about to occur is awareness. Try asking, "What possibility am I avoiding with the *uncomfortable* I am choosing?"

Uncomfortable is just an awareness of change, my friend. That's all it is. Stop trying to make yourself comfortable and start enjoying the misery. You've defined *uncomfortable* as miserable and *comfort* as an unawareness that works for you.

MT:

Can we change that?

Gary:

No, you have to *choose* it. You have to look at it and say, "You know what? Enough of this. This is crap. If I were choosing my reality, what would I choose?" That's the question. That's the one thing that will get you out of it. All of you have to do this. You have to start asking: "If I were choosing my reality what would I choose?" You've got to start choosing your reality—because if you don't, you're doomed.

MT:

I think I must have misapplied and misidentified comfort with ease.

Gary:

You *assume*, which makes an ass out of you and me, that if you have ease, you won't have discomfort. You don't get that if you have discomfort, it is only an awareness of what you have not yet been willing to receive.

MT:

Can you say that again?

Gary:

It doesn't matter how many times I say it, you're not going to hear it.

MT:

One more time, please.

*If you have discomfort, it is only an awareness of
what you have not yet been willing to receive.*

BEING A COMFORT JUNKIE

Gary:

When you are aware of discomfort, it is the moment before success begins. You think it is easier not to be successful so you can be a comfort junkie.

MT:

So how do I change that? Is it just a choice?

Gary:

It's all a creation. What would happen if you went to "Wow, what's about to happen that I'm not comfortable with?" If you get clear that you are willing to have that discomfort and realize something is about to occur that you haven't been expecting or that you haven't been willing to receive, you won't say, "Oh my God, this is terrible. I want to go back to comfort." You will never choose comfort. You will choose possibility above all things.

MT:

What's coming up for me is discomfort and pain. The word *pain* keeps coming up.

Gary:

Have you ever actually had pain?

MT:

No.

Gary:

That's because you are a comfort junkie. Anything that would create pain, you would never allow to happen.

GN:

I may be a comfort junkie as well.

Gary:

You think you are comfortable as long as your wife is not angry with you.

GN:

Yes, and to a point that works. But it also becomes a major limitation of never going to what's beyond the discomfort.

Gary:

That's right. That's what comfort junkies suffer from. They never go beyond where comfort lives. They never go beyond their greatest limitation. It's just a choice.

GN:

Absolutely.

PR:

So if you get uncomfortable right before you have the change and you...

Gary:

I didn't say, "change." I said, "Before something great occurs."

PR:

Once the greatness occurs, does that bring comfort to the discomfort?

Gary:

Wow, you're doing a great job of trying to come to conclusion about whether you are going to experience discomfort or be a comfort junkie. You are trying to decide what you are going to do before you get there, which is not possible. Before you have an orgasm, do you decide what it's going to be before you choose it?

PR:

Good point.

Gary:

And sometimes it's not terribly comfortable just before you achieve an orgasm. Have you noticed?

PR:

Yes.

Gary:

Sometimes it's like "Okay, harder, faster, quicker," sometimes it's "No, slow down, slow down." Sometimes it's "Oh my god, am I going to survive this?" I'm trying to give you guys a reference point you can receive.

PR:

It's brilliant the way you are saying it. I see that my question is "What is comfort and what is discomfort?"

Gary:

Discomfort is a level of intensity that you have decided you cannot receive. I don't have the point of view that there's anything I can't receive so it doesn't matter how uncomfortable it is. I ask, "Okay, what's this going to create?"

PR:

That's the part that has been missing for me, Gary. "What's this going to create?" rather than going to "Ahhh."

Gary:

You guys keep trying to go to "Ahhh." That's why you are comfort junkies. You don't get to the "Ahhh" because you say, "Oh, I can handle this" or "Oh, that was nice." That was *nice!* Where's *fabulous?* Where's *phenomenance* in the scheme of things?

LM:

Can you say what comfort I am avoiding?

Gary:

I know this happens to be your item, which is why you are having a problem. It's a dilemma as it were. Sitting there and doing nothing is the comfort junkie position: "Okay good, I'm not going to do anything; that way I won't actually have to learn anything." You have to use whatever you've got available to you instead of refusing it. You tend to refuse so you can keep the comfort you've decided is greater than your ability to create.

Everything that is times a godzillion, will you destroy and uncreate it all? Right and Wrong, Good and Bad, POD and POC, All 9, Shorts, Boys, and Beyonds.

MT:

I have a question, but I might get in trouble if I ask it.

Gary:

That would not be a question. That would be "Can I blame my wife?" And you will get in trouble for that one. Deservedly so. She doesn't stop you from anything. You stop yourself. I can guarantee you that if I ask her if she can stop you from anything, she will say, "Well, I try." And how well does that work? It doesn't. Nobody stops you from doing anything except you. And you're better at it than anybody. You'd rather stop you than have the discomfort of creating as you.

Everything that is times a godzillion, will you destroy and uncreate it all? Right and Wrong, Good and Bad, POD and POC, All 9, Shorts, Boys, and Beyonds. Okay, yeah you want something else?

Your point of view creates your lack of comfort, not reality.

MT:

Is it that I have bought that *comfortable* is more valuable than *uncomfortable?*

Gary:

You've bought that *comfortable* is more valuable than *awareness.*

MT:

Can we change that?

Gary:

No. You've got to keep it that way forever.

MT:

No.

Gary:

What kind of comfort is "No"?

Everything you have done to create comfort as greater than awareness, will you destroy and uncreate all that? Right and Wrong, Good and Bad, POD and POC, All 9, Shorts, Boys, and Beyonds.

What have you made so vital about comfort that you will refuse awareness in order to achieve it? Everything that is times a godzillion, will you destroy and uncreate it all? Right and Wrong, Good and Bad, POD and POC, All 9, Shorts, Boys, and Beyonds.

So have you chosen awareness, or have you chosen comfort?

MT:

Comfort comes up.

Gary:

Everywhere you've chosen comfort over awareness will you destroy and uncreate all that? Right and Wrong, Good and Bad, POD and POC, All 9, Shorts, Boys, and Beyonds.

What have you made so vital about comfort that you would give up awareness in order to achieve it? This is, by the way, one of those achievable states. The state of achievement is comfort. And you would want that for what reason? Everything that is times a godzillion, will you destroy and uncreate it all? Right and Wrong, Good and Bad, POD and POC, All 9, Shorts, Boys, and Beyonds.

You're not allowed to blame your wife for anything anymore. You're not allowed to justify what you don't choose based on your wife's point of view. Everything that is times a godzillion, will you destroy and uncreate it all? Right and Wrong, Good and Bad, POD and POC, All 9, Shorts, Boys, and Beyonds.

If you go seeking comfort, what you don't do is create massive amounts of wealth, massive amounts of choices, or massive amounts of possibility. You can live a little tiny life, happy in your 1,000 square meter house, thinking you are living elegantly and fabulously.

What have you made so vital about comfort that you would give up all awareness in order to keep it? Everything that is times a godzillion, will you destroy and uncreate it all? Right and Wrong, Good and Bad, POD and POC, All 9, Shorts, Boys, and Beyonds.

Where did you guys buy the idea that awareness is not comfortable and it's not valuable and it's going to get in the way of your having a sense of comfort? Everywhere you bought that, will you destroy and uncreate it all and return it to sender with consciousness attached? Right and Wrong, Good and Bad, POD and POC, All 9, Shorts, Boys, and Beyonds.

What have you made so vital about comfort that you would give up awareness in order to achieve it?

NM:

For me, awareness is uncomfortable because I have to look at how people are functioning and the choices they make.

Gary:

Why is that uncomfortable?

NM:

Because I can see greater possibilities.

Gary:

And you don't want to see greater possibilities? You'd rather be comfortable?

NM:

It's uncomfortable to see the choices my family members are making.

Gary:

You say it is uncomfortable, but isn't it actually irritating to you to realize that people are creating something that is a crock of shit?

NM:

Irritating, yes, but it is more than irritating.

Gary:

Yeah, it's "How stupid can they be?" And that is not really a question. It's a statement, "My family is stupid." The question would be "How crazy can they be? And how unaware?"

NM:

I see that I'm using that as an excuse to not be aware because it is uncomfortable to see what they are choosing.

Gary:

Yes, I know. When you see what they're choosing, you have to say, "Oh, interesting choice." You want to have comfort, so instead of doing "interesting point of view" about your family's point of view, which would give you true comfort, you take that point of view and try to hide it from yourself.

NM:

Exactly.

Gary:

That's like a good Easter egg. One year I did such a good job of hiding Easter eggs that my kids couldn't find them all, and four Easter eggs rotted in our house and started to smell. That was not nice. That's when I gave up hiding them well and started hiding them obviously, because I didn't want to smell that ever again. That was discomfort to me.

What have you made so vital about comfort that you would give up all awareness in order to keep it? Everything that is times a godzillion, will you destroy and uncreate it all? Right and Wrong, Good and Bad, POD and POC, All 9, Shorts, Boys, and Beyonds.

You want to have comfort, so instead of doing "interesting point of view" about your family's point of view, which would give you true comfort, you take that point of view and try to hide it from yourself.

BEING A DISCOMFORT JUNKIE

KC:
Gary, is there such a thing as being a *discomfort* junkie?

Gary:
Yeah. That's based on the idea that you need to have something outside of you that will motivate you. You do discomfort to motivate yourself to do or change something. Cute, don't you think? You need to have something to complain about or you don't see any reason to change anything. What if you just realized that you had infinite choice and asked, "What would I like to change today?" I get up in the morning wondering what I would like to change.

I don't ask, "What do I have to do?" or "Where's my *do-do* list for today?" Rather, I ask, "What would I like to change or create today that would be fun for me? Who could I mess with in wonderful ways?"

ND:

What's the difference between being a discomfort junkie and being willing to do whatever it takes and feels as uncomfortable as necessary?

Gary:

If you use discomfort as a way of changing something, you are a discomfort junkie. If you are willing to do whatever it takes to get whatever you want, then you are an aggressive junkie. You like being aggressive. You want to change things, you want to do things, and you don't want to wait. How many of you have spent your life on "wait"? It's always a good thing to do. Be a waiter in your own life: "When this happens, then I will …. When this occurs, then I will …." I don't wait for anything or anyone. I create every single, solitary, frigging day.

> *"What would I like to change or create today*
> *that would be fun for me?*
> *Who could I mess with in wonderful ways?"*

FIGHTING FOR YOUR POINT OF VIEW

NE:

I was having some really intense energy and I thought, "I need to find somebody to trade body processes with." I went to the back of the room where Dain was and I said, "I need somebody to trade with." Dain said, "What? I thought you said, 'I need somebody to fight with.'"

I said, "No, no, no. I'm not looking for anyone to fight with." But this thing of wanting to fight has been really prevalent in my universe.

Gary:

How much of your life have you had to fight for your point of view? Do you think that if you don't fight you can't have your point of view?

Everything that is times a godzillion, will you destroy and uncreate it all? Right and Wrong, Good and Bad, POD and POC, All 9, Shorts, Boys, and Beyonds.

When you make it your reality that you have to fight for your point of view, or you have to fight for your awareness, or you have to fight for what you want to have in life, you set up "I must fight to get, to have, to create, and to generate." What if that's not going to get you what you want? Fighting for something means you have to find somebody who is in opposition to your having it, which means you can't have the people who will have your back and help you create it.

You all know that you are very tough. You're all saying, "In my reality, I'm tough."

How many of you have tried to be tough and mean? Real meanness is stinginess with self.

How's that working for you?

What if, instead of being tough or mean, you were totally aware and willing to manipulate anybody who got in your way? Everything that is times a godzillion, will you destroy and uncreate it all? Right and Wrong, Good and Bad, POD and POC, All 9, Shorts, Boys, and Beyonds.

How much of your life have you had to fight
for your point of view?
Do you think that if you don't fight you can't have
your point of view?

ACKNOWLEDGING YOUR REALITY

TR:

The more you talk, the more I see that I have a reality I haven't acknowledged myself for. How can I keep that acknowledgement going?

Gary:

You can't lose something when you acknowledge it. When you acknowledge it, it is yours forever. You only lose it when you try to see somebody else's point of view about it.

LM:

Are you saying that some of us have no reality?

Gary:

That's correct. It's kind of a shock, isn't it? Most of you try to figure out how you can function in this reality because that means you finally have your reality.

LM:

I thought we all had some sort of reality.

Gary:

Most people consider they have their reality when they fight against somebody else's point of view. To them fighting means they have a reality, but fighting has nothing to do with creating a reality. Reality is about creation. And when you don't create from your reality, you buy into this reality and become a slave to it.

LM:

Do I have to be totally aware of my reality before I can change it or improve it or alter it?

Gary:

You don't have to be totally aware, but you do have to have some idea of what your reality is. "Where is my reality?" is a good question to begin with. Ask:

+ What is my reality?
+ What would I not give up to have my reality?

The thing you would give up to keep what you call your reality is the one thing that is keeping you from having your reality.

CW:

You said I have to choose my own reality. I thought I was doing that. I get to work with amazing people like you, I get to travel with my work...

Gary:

That is part of your reality, but you keep overriding what you are creating. Do you honor the fact that you create miracles? That would be a *no*. Do you acknowledge the fact that you have had successes there is no way to explain? Are you aware that you have been able to pull off some phenomenal stuff in the newspapers in Brisbane for the Antique Guild that other antique stores were so envious of they could hardly stand it?

Your reality is going out, contacting people, and creating things that other people can't create, and you keep assuming that those things occur because you do things like other people do. But you don't do things the way other people do, and you get results that other people can't get. I am trying to help you see what your reality is, but you guys keep finding ways to reject it.

Nothing occurs in your life. You create it.

WHAT'S RELEVANT TO YOU?

BH:

You have talked about how people make their reality relative to others and how it doesn't work to do that. I have done that with a friend, and I question whether it's working.

But when I make things relevant to you or my sister, it usually puts me into something that's very spacious. Whenever I am lost, confused, weird, or wonky, I know I need to talk to you, my sister, or KN.

Gary:

Yes, but that's creating your own reality. You're realizing who is relevant to your life. The people who create spaciousness in your life are the people you want to have as vital to your life.

BH:

That's what happens when I talk to you. I gain the relevance of my reality.

Gary:

Exactly. Most relationships are about how you avoid the relevance of your reality. You diminish what is relevant to you in favor of what is relevant to the other person and their point of view.

BH:

Do you see where I am diminishing what is relevant to me in relationship to anybody?

Gary:

The only place I see you making you less is by your conclusions. "I don't want to do that" is the primary one you choose. That's what you make relative, and it keeps you away from what is truly relevant to you.

BH:

Today when we were sitting and talking…

Gary:

I suggested you do a television program, and you said, "I don't want to do that!"

BH:

Yes, I do that, and there is more that I have made relevant.

Gary:

You make things relevant to what people can currently receive.

BH:

I don't think that's what it is for me.

Gary:

That is what it is.

BH:

Okay, I have made it relevant to what other people can create. Definitely.

Gary:

You have made it relevant what other people are putting out in the world.

BH:

Because if I get on TV and talk about the things I talk about… There is nothing like it. It is just total crazy time. To me it seems normal, but I can see that those things, spoken on a world stage, would be like…

Gary:

Yes, but that's the phenomenance you have to be. That's the phenomenance for changing the world and creating a different reality. I am willing to be seen as the nut job of the Western world. I am willing to be the nut job that everyone rejects or thinks is horrible.

BH:

And I won't.

Gary:

You won't. You're still making your reality relative to what will create some kind of apparency of "normal."

BH:

Yeah, and I don't want people to dislike me.

Gary:

I was thrilled today to find out the Pope doesn't like me. Apparently a Catholic women's organization has put something out that says we are dangerous. I consider that one of the nicest things I have heard in years.

BH:

That's because you think that people not liking you is a favor they are doing you. I have not made that transition yet.

Gary:

No, you just haven't made that choice yet.

CL:

With what BH is saying, I was watching some YouTube videos the other day and I noticed that the video you made on "Right Voice for You" now has over 4.8 million views. Any time someone searches "amazing singer," it is one of the first things that come up.

Gary:

That's funny.

CL:

I watched it, and you are POD and POCing the whole time. You are wiggling your fingers and destroying past lifetimes, projections, and expectations. There are thousands of comments. People are divided about whether you changed anything and the singer got better, but nobody is saying, "That is so weird." They are making comments like "This coach is amazing."

Gary:

Or "This guy is ridiculous. He's not doing anything."

CL:

Or "Nothing happened," but there is almost no energy on *how* you did it—only whether it worked or not. In my radio shows, I POD and POC things, and in my classes I do absolutely whatever, but I have decided something about videos. A lot of my videos look really "normal."

Gary:

You have made your videos relative to what you have decided people can receive. Anywhere you make something relative to what you have decided people can receive, it's always your judgment of what they can receive rather than an opportunity for them to receive a different possibility.

CL:

And nothing about that is weird to you. Or you don't care if people see it as weird.

Gary:

People don't see what I do as weird because I don't see it as weird. It's just "This is what I do. You like it, great; you don't like it, great. Whatever makes you happy."

CL:

I would like to have more of that.

Gary:

You won't stand out from the crowd and POD and POC in your videos because you make it relevant that people will judge you. Stop making your choices based on what is relative to other people's realities. Never make a choice based on other people's realities.

CL:

I have bought using a gentler way to get people interested in Access. And there may be some truth to that.

Gary:

I don't know. I put myself out on a limb at all times and the strangest frigging things happen. When you make it gentler, you make it relative to the idea there is something wrong with Access, which is a judgment.

GG:

BH, there are people who travel all around New Zealand doing shows where they talk to dead people and give messages to living people who are more dead than they are. They fill all the halls. I listened to a guy from England who talked about this stuff in the biggest theatre we have, and it was packed. Everyone was crying. They bought boxes of tissues. You are not weird in this country.

I used to not do weird stuff in my clinic because everyone in the clinic thought I was strange. They would listen at the door to hear what was going on. A lady came to see me who had a knee operation, and she was cranky. I could see it in every part of her being. I asked her, "What's going on? Why are you grumpy?"

She said, "I'm not grumpy."

I said, "The scar on your knee is red and angry. What are you angry about?"

She said, "It's taking too frigging long to heal."

I said, "If you love your knee and you're grateful for it, watch that disappear the scar. And watch the mobility come back." The next week she and her daughter came back. They are loud, outspoken, big women. They had silly smirks on their faces, and they called me a weird bastard. The mum got on the table and I moved her trousers up to the top of the thigh and there was a white line where the angry redness had been. I said, "Well, didn't you do good!"

She said, "No, you did it."

I said, "Nah, nah, nah, you can take the weirdness this time."

Now whenever they come into the clinic, they want me to work on them because I'm the one who does weird stuff.

Gary:

That's what you've got to do. You've got to *not* have it relative to what people can receive. It's got to be relevant to *you*, whether it is relevant to anybody else or not. If you live from what is relevant to you, you are always being truthful with the world. And the one thing that is irresistible to people is someone who speaks what is true for them.

BH:

Maybe you can help me with this piece about what GG was saying because I agree that psychic mediumship and fortune telling are more or less acceptable in the world now.

Gary:

Well, you are just a step beyond that.

BH:

Help me with this piece because the actualization of living in a world… I am noticing that people will get all the way through the "Talk to the Entities" Advanced Class and they will say, "Holy shit! I am aware of entities!" They want to come to the class and have me tell them the story, but they don't want to see the story themselves. But if you come and do my class, you are going to be in relationship with entities.

Gary:

And the problem is?

BH:

Thank you. There isn't a problem. What is this thing I am aware of, because there is huge... energy... that's the best thing I can call it.

Gary:

What did you come here to do? To open the door to people getting the reality of this?

BH:

Yeah. I guess so.

Gary:

So if that's why you came here, why aren't you doing it?

BH:

I'm getting there.

Gary:

I know, but you're not willing to put yourself out in the world. You keep looking at what you do as relative to *other people*, not how it is relevant to you.

BH:

Wow.

Gary:

That's the thing CL was talking about. I do what is relevant to me. I don't give a damn how people see me, talk about me, or anything else.

BH:

I am not trying to be contrary, but I don't give that much of a damn, either. Am I lying to myself?

Gary:

Well, you just stated it. You said, "I don't give that much of a damn." You give a little damn.

BH:

Okay, somewhere I give a little damn.

NE:

I think I have been making people relevant because I don't want them to feel bad.

Gary:

That makes you a very good hostess. You should be on an airplane.

NE:

The true gift is making *me* relevant. Being my reality here.

Gary:

Yes, it's doing what's relevant to you and not worrying about what other people think. It's like CL said, four million people have seen that YouTube video.

CL:

Four point eight million. It had an extra 800,000 views in the last couple of weeks. It's like a Jennifer Lopez video.

Gary:

Some people look at the YouTube video and they say, "This is great." They send it to their friends and say, "You have to watch this." The people who don't like it don't send it to anybody. As it grows and more people watch it, more people send it to their friends, and more people will like it than not like it.

If you live from what is relevant to you, you are always being truthful with the world.

BEING AN AUTHORITY

NE:

Am I not willing to make this human reality irrelevant?

Gary:

It's not that you have to make it irrelevant. You just don't make it relevant to *you*. You have to get what's relevant to you. You guys have the point of view that you have to make this reality irrelevant in order to have your relevance. No. You just need to see what's relevant to you and do that. Whether it is relevant to anybody else is irrelevant. It's what's relevant to you that counts.

Do you know how much energy you are using against what you say you want? You say you want to create more consciousness, but in order to create more consciousness, you have to be an authority out in the world, because then people will listen to what you say and be interested in what you say.

I am an authority whether anybody else gets it or not.
I am an authority by my reality not by anybody else's. If
other people make me an authority, fine. If they don't,
fine. It doesn't matter to me. I am only interested in "How
do I become the authority in the world that creates more
consciousness?"

I realized that I could create all of the consciousness I
wanted sitting at home, but unless I got myself out in the
world and became an authority...

How many of you are doing everything you can to
avoid becoming an authority out in the world so you can
avoid the success and infinite possibilities you could be
choosing? Everything that is times a godzillion, will you
destroy and uncreate it all? Right and Wrong, Good and
Bad, POD and POC, All 9, Shorts, Boys, and Beyonds.

NE:

Do you see anything else that might be in my way of that?

Gary:

Just the willingness to be successful.

What have you made so vital about never possessing
the phenomenance of success in the world that would
make you an authority for the creation of more
consciousness? Everything that is times a godzillion,
will you destroy and uncreate it all? Right and Wrong,
Good and Bad, POD and POC, All 9, Shorts, Boys, and
Beyonds.

You guys say you want consciousness, but you are avoiding the one thing that would create consciousness, which is choosing relative to you.

What have you made so vital about never possessing the phenomenance of success in the world out there that would make you an authority for the creation of more consciousness? Everything that is times a godzillion, will you destroy and uncreate it all? Right and Wrong, Good and Bad, POD and POC, All 9, Shorts, Boys, and Beyonds.

You just need to see what's relevant to you and do that.
Whether it is relevant to anybody else is irrelevant.

CREATING YOUR REALITY RELATIVE TO OTHERS

At one point when I was working with Dain, he saw that he was trying to create his reality relative to the things he had learned from the people around him. He had a mother who believed she should be with women, he had a grandmother who believed that everything sexual was wrong, and he had a father who believed that all women were things to be used. Dain came away with a confusion about what his point of view was, because everything he decided was relative to his mother's, grandmother's, and father's point of view.

How many of your points of view have you taken relative to someone else, which are not even relative to you? Everything that is times a godzillion, will you

destroy and uncreate it all? Right and Wrong, Good and Bad, POD and POC, All 9, Shorts, Boys, and Beyonds.

People do this in business all the time. They make their business relative to x, y, or z. They say, "Well, our success is relative to this. Our success will be relative to commanding these people in the world. Our success will be relative to...."

You have to know what is relevant to you personally as a form of success. Have any of you determined what your reality is with regard to success? No, you haven't. And then you wonder why you have no success. You have always made success relative to somebody else's point of view—not what is relevant to you. You look for what is relative to how something will affect others or how others will receive you or how others will judge you. You do not do what is relevant to you. You have to choose what's relevant to you—not how it has to be by somebody else's reality.

Everything that is times a godzillion, will you destroy and uncreate it all? Right and Wrong, Good and Bad, POD and POC, All 9, Shorts, Boys, and Beyonds.

AK:

My mother used to come into my room every morning and say, "Rise and shine. A new day dawns with opportunities for you to better yourself." When you said that thing about success, I realized I could never have success because I always had to better myself. So I'm stealing your definition of success, which is "If I change one person, I am a success."

Gary:

If I change one person in the world, it's a better place.

LM:

I have to be busy all the time. I think I picked that up from my family. There are so many things I have to do, and I just can't get through everything. I wrote twenty-five things down on my list and I thought I'd tick them off as I completed each one. I did that and in the meantime I got a few extras that I added on.

Gary:

You have a *do-do* list. When you have a do-do list, every time you tick one item off you add two more. Pretty soon you have a three page do-do list. As long as you have a do-do list, you are a do-do head. What if you were a be-be head instead? Where's your *be-be* list?

PN:

What's a be-be list?

Gary:

"What am I going *to be* today? How many things can I *be* today?"

CW:

And how could I have fun with that?

Gary:

Well, don't do that, because that might be your reality!
    You make everything in your reality relative to something other than your choice and what is truly

relevant to you. What have you made relative that keeps the distance between you and what is relevant to you as your reality? Everything that is times a godzillion, will you destroy and uncreate it all? Right and Wrong, Good and Bad, POC and POD, All 9, Shorts, Boys, and Beyonds.

AK:

Is that an addiction to reference points?

Gary:

No, that is an addiction to believing that other people have something to offer and you have nothing to offer. Be less mean to you. Show up for you not for other people. You have made everything about the relationship or the relativity to other people, not about you. You've got to have your reality. You have to ask: "What's actually relevant for me? What do I want to create and do?"

The gift you are is the energy of being you. When you are that, you change the energies of everything around you. That's the gift you actually are.

> *You have to know what is relevant to you*
> *personally as a form of success.*

ALL THAT YOU ARE

DT:

Could you talk about the ease of being? When you step into the phenomenance of having your own reality, is that when you have the ease of being?

Gary:

You step into phenomenance when the ease of being becomes the dominant species of your own reality. The phenomenance of having your own reality gives you the place where you can create anything. Do you want to create or do you want to vegetate? You have had your own reality and you have created a lot, haven't you?

DT:

Yes.

Gary:

Have you created more in the last six years than you did in the previous six years?

DT:

Yes.

Gary:

Do you think the next six years will be less productive or more productive?

DT:

More productive. And at the same time, I still don't have the ease of being.

Gary:

Yes, because you have not yet claimed all that you are. But you will.

DT:

What would it take?

Gary:

You will, don't worry.

DT:

Thank you.

You have not yet claimed all that you are. But you will.

BEING YOU AND CREATING YOUR REALITY

NM:

Am I holding onto LM in some way? I'm wondering if I am holding onto his strangeness and trying to control him.

Gary:

Enjoy his strangeness, because it's the gift of living he has. Nobody has ever been able to stop him from being as odd as he is. That's a good thing. You've got one of the strangest men on the planet and you are trying to create him as an average kind of guy.

NM:

Yes.

LM:

I'm sorry.

Gary:

Don't be sorry! Be glad about that. When you are sorry about what you are, you have to diminish you so you look normal instead of being as strange as you are.

NM:

I am trying to hold onto being normal, aren't I?

Gary:

Yes, you are trying desperately to hold onto some kind of normal. You think that phenomenance is being normal.

What have you made so vital about the phenomenance of normal, average, real, and the same as everybody else that keeps you from the strangeness of total creation you could be? "Creative people are strange. They're weird. You've got to be careful about them." Everything that is times a godzillion, will you destroy and uncreate it all? Right and Wrong, Good and Bad, POD and POC, All 9, Shorts, Boys, and Beyonds.

To be normal, average, real, and the same as everybody else is phenomenal for you, because that is so hard for you. It's as if you think that anybody who is normal, average, and real must be phenomenal because being that is so much work.

NM:

Yes, that is a lot of work.

Gary:

You are working really hard to be normal, average, and real because you think that's phenomenance. No, that's *limitation.* That's all that is.

Everything that is times a godzillion, will you destroy and uncreate it all? Right and Wrong, Good and Bad, POD and POC, All 9, Shorts, Boys, and Beyonds.

It's trying to fit into what everybody else is instead of asking, "What can I create that is so different

that I succeed beyond anybody else's wildest reality?" When you talk to the people here, haven't

you seen how amazing some of them are? Almost all of them are—except the ones who are trying hard to be normal, average, real, and the same as everybody else. And when you talk to them, you always know they are lying and you say, "Uh, boring," and you go talk to somebody else.

What have you made so vital about possessing the phenomenance of normal, average, real, and the same as everybody else that keeps you from creating a reality beyond this reality? Everything that is times a godzillion, will you destroy and uncreate it all? Right and Wrong, Good and Bad, POD and POC, All 9, Shorts, Boys, and Beyonds.

Most people are trying so hard to be normal, average, and real. They think that's phenomenal.

They think they want to become extraordinary, which is extra-of-the-ordinary, but that's not being all the things that they can be. It's not being phenomenal. I want to make you guys step up to what you don't want to step up to, whether you like it or not.

NM:

Thank you.

When you are sorry about what you are,
you have to diminish you so you look normal
instead of being as strange as you are.

"IF I WERE CREATING MY REALITY, WHAT WOULD I CHOOSE ?"

TS:

During this conversation, I've been looking at "What is it that I am not choosing or creating? Am I not willing to have responsibility?" But that's not it. It's about the willingness to include me and create my reality.

Gary:

Yes, creating your reality requires you to practice every day. You have to ask the question, "If I were creating my reality, what would I choose?" Most of us create this reality from "I've got kids so I've got to do this. I've got a business so I've got to do that." What we need to ask is: "If I were creating my reality, what would I choose here?"

TS:

That's the greatest kindness.

Gary:

Yes, that's the greatest kindness to you. That will also give you everything you want in life. You will have contentment with the fact that you are creating that much. The greatest joy in life is the contentment of creation.

TS:

Creating at a bigger level is turning me on. And being willing to be that kind. Being a walking, talking orgasm.

Gary:

Yeah, you get to be the walking, talking orgasm you truly be, which would be that place of always being expansive.

Creating your reality requires you to practice every day.

The Phenomenance of Creation

PR:

I had a beautiful session this morning from Dain. I had an "aha" moment: Being you requires no effort at all. That's the one thing that has true ease, joy, and glory—you being you. There is no significance to you being you … at all.

Gary:

No. It's just a choice.

PR:

You don't have to try.

Gary:

That's the phenomenance of creation. Knowing that what gets created today is going to create something tomorrow. What's it going to create? What's it going to look like? What am I going to have to deliver then when it shows up? This is the phenomenance of creation. You never look for just handling now. You look at how to handle everything now and in the future.

THE BLESSED POSSIBILITY OF WHAT CAN EXIST

DT:

You've talked about the way people in New Zealand are super laid-back and seem to ooze through life. I sense that when you are being phenomenance, you can still ooze through life. Is that right?

Gary:

Yes, when you are in phenomenance, you ooze through life without the necessity of fighting for or against anything in order to create. Creation then becomes the phenomenance of choice.

DT:

What's the difference between that and the people who ooze without creating?

Gary:

They have misidentified and misapplied that ease means they don't need to create. So if they create anything, they create the smallest possible thing they can create, thinking that's enough. And it *is* enough, because they don't need much. But they could create so much more. They could create so much more phenomenance in the world.

DT:

So they would have phenomenance in conjunction with oozing, because you can't have struggle and phenomenance?

Gary:

If you are doing struggle, you are not doing phenomenance. But that doesn't mean that you have to ooze through life. It can be that there's a desire to accomplish more than anybody else is willing to accomplish. For example, when you start to write a book, you usually end up writing three of them. Have you noticed? That's the phenomenance of creation. When you are functioning from the phenomenance of creation, you don't function from a conclusion about what you have to create before you create. You start creating and you realize what else becomes possible as a result of the moment of creation that is stimulating you all the time to be and do more than anybody else will ever be and do.

DT:

And that moment of creation is oozing for me?

Gary:

Well, it oozes into your awareness, through your awareness, and into the world, not as something you have to impel on the world but as something that is an acoustical vibration of the possibility. It's the blessed possibility of what can exist.

If you are doing struggle, you are not doing phenomenance.

BE THE INSPIRATION TO CREATION

MP:

How do we inspire people to make that next step into creation?

Gary:

Many people think inspiration means doing something for someone else. I never do anything for anyone else. I do it for me. And in being willing to choose things that other people won't choose, I inspire people to choose more than they ever thought they could choose. When I was in Venice, we went to a flea market and I bought some lamps to send to the Antique Guild in Brisbane. I could see the beauty in them. DT looked at them and said, "Oh." She couldn't see the beauty of them at all. Later, when she saw a picture of them in the Guild, she said, "Wow, they *are* beautiful."

Be the inspiration by being the joy and watch how many people choose to get happier and to create more because of your willingness to be joyful and happy. Your willingness to be joyful and happy is the beginning of stepping into the phenomenance, because you are not defining what it is you are supposed to do or how you are supposed to do it.

People in Access inspire others all the time with the books they write, the classes they give, the things they do, and the gifts they have and be. Donnielle Carter is an inspiration with "Right Body for You." Is she a super-skinny model/ movie star kind of girl? No. She is simply being the joy of her body—and that inspires people. Before she went to do a body class in Australia, she said, "I'm just going to have fun.

Whatever happens, whatever judgment there might be, I am just going to have a good time." She has been overwhelmed and touched by the response from the classes she did there, and I have received so many emails from people who said how grateful they were for her classes. One person said, "I came away with a level of comfort in my body that I have never had in my life."

Among the many people who have written inspiring books about Access, two people stand out at the moment: Anne Maxwell, who wrote a book with us called *You Wouldn't Teach a Fish to Climb a Tree*, which is about kids who have ADD, ADHD, OCD, and autism. She loves working with those kids, and she is a total inspiration. I recently got an email from a lady who said, "I'm a seventy-five-year-old fish. Thank you for showing me that I don't have to climb a tree." Liam Phillips has inspired people with his book, *Curing the Incurable*. There are people who haven't died because of him.

FB:

You have said that you create in order to inspire, but I always thought it was the other way around. I've always thought that you required inspiration in order to create.

Gary:

No, you don't require inspiration to create. You create because it inspires you. You create to inspire yourself. Did you notice that you got really excited about bringing antique jewelry here to show people? When I asked you about bringing the jewelry, you said, "Oh yes! I want to come, I want to do this!"

I said, "You don't have to."

And you said, "No, no! I want to!"

I said, "Really, you don't have to."

And you said, "But I want to!"

FB:

I am confused.

Gary:

What have you made so vital about never being the phenomenance of creation that keeps you from being the inspiration? Everything that is times a godzillion, will you destroy and uncreate it all? Right and Wrong, Good and Bad, POD and POC, All 9, Shorts, Boys, and Beyonds.

> *You don't require inspiration to create.*
> *You create because it inspires you.*

INSPIRING PEOPLE TO A DIFFERENT POSSIBILITY

Several of you have mentioned fracking and Fukushima. What would happen with fracking and Fukushima and all the craziness going on in the world if you were willing to stop fighting it and ask:

- What could I create that would inspire people to a different possibility?
- What could I be that would create something different here?
- What could I be that would create a different possibility?

What could you create that would inspire other people? You need to out-create the insanity, not fight it. Fighting the insanity only makes the insanity stronger. Out-creating it disbands its foundation of existence.

I recently had a conversation with Marilyn Bradford about "Right Recovery for You." She said, "No one seems to want to deal with the things I talk about concerning addiction."

I said, "That's because nobody wants to admit that they are an addict. People are addicted to the trauma, drama, upset, and intrigue, but that's not what you need to talk about. You have to talk about how they recover. It's called Right Recovery for You. Focus on the *recovery*. Talk about how they recover, not the addiction. It's a different story."

Never talk to people about how they are crippled, because that's what they will fixate on. Talk to their desire. Always speak to people's desire. It's about the phenomenance of following what you know is true for you and good for you. When you do that, everything falls into place. It just comes together. You don't have to fight anything.

MA:

This also applies to a project I'm working on, "Education for a Conscious Future." There are a lot of people who want to talk about the trauma and drama of the educational system, but I don't see that as the way to go.

Gary:

You have to ask them, "If you were in charge of the schools, what would you change in order to make them better?"

Then people will give you their ideas. And from their ideas, you could write a book that will create something amazing.

MA:

That's awesome. Thank you.

Gary:

People complain about things, but they don't inspire a different possibility. They just complain about what is. They are talking about what's crippled; they are not talking to the possibility. You have to ask:

- What's actually possible here that we haven't considered?
- Where do we go from here?
- Where is it possible for us to go that we haven't gone?

FB:

I'm getting how creation is what inspires me and how you often speak to that desire in me. How can I be more of that with my team?

Gary:

You could ask them:

- If you were creating this business to be highly successful, what would you do?
- What would you do to create this business as so successful that you could never lose your job?

FB:

Oh, that is funny!

Gary:

You are doing two things with that. You're scaring the shit out of them and encouraging them to choose to be aware. Most people only do a job until they lose it. Or they take a job and sort of work at it. They don't do a bad job but they don't create. Inspire your team to create by asking them: "If you were creating this all on your own, what would you do that would be beyond anything you have ever chosen that would create magnificently?"

FB:

That's a whole different style of leadership!

What could I create that would inspire people to
a different possibility?

THE GIFT YOU HAVE IS
THE DIFFERENCE YOU ARE

JT:

In my industry, it's important that people respect me, pay attention to what I'm doing, and copy it. I like to inspire people. I want to get my work out into the world, where it is bigger with the public.

Gary:

In order to inspire people, you have to be willing to know what your reality is and go there, regardless of anybody else's point of view. Is this making sense to you? You have to get this because it will increase your presence. Be the rocking presence you can be.

You keep acquiescing to other people's needs, requires, or desires and giving up you in favor of their point of view. Is that going to create the result you are looking for in life?

JT:

No.

Gary:

Ask: "What's going to create the result I want in life?"

You think that you need to be *not* different than others. I'm sorry to tell you this, but you came in different from other people. And if you use that difference, you can create far more. I recently saw a documentary on the designer Gianni Versace. He came in as a little kid who loved wearing dresses. He went to school to become an architect or something like that and he failed. He was on the football team and it wasn't working. He finally got that he was not straight and he became willing to be outrageous when other people wouldn't. Once he did that, he became a guru of fashion.

You can be a guru of possibilities in your industry if you are willing to be outrageous enough. But you can't continue to withdraw yourself from life and from others, because when you do that, people can't receive what you can be. You keep refusing to be everything you are. It's a matter of choice.

There is an unkindness when you are not being everything you are. It's the unkindness of not being you. When you're not being you, other people can't see you. They can't see what you are trying to inspire them to. You are actually denying people the inspiration and the choice of possibility.

Each one of you has the ability to be something you are not being. If you chose to be that, you would give other people the inspiration to create, generate, and be something greater than they have been willing to be, which would generate and create a different planet, a different Earth.

What do you want to create? Do you want to create the same old shit? Then keep withdrawing. Do you want to create a different reality? Then step up and show up! Be the inspiration by being the difference you are. Be that and you inspire people. When you don't *be* that, you are being mean in every way. You are being penurious. You are holding onto what you have as though nobody else can have it. That is not being kind.

The gift you have is the difference you are.
Be that and you inspire people.

HOW ARE YOU GOING TO CHANGE THE WORLD?

VT:

When JT needs or desires to be taken care of, I say, "That's fine," and I take care of her. When I do that, am I limiting the possibility for her to be the phenomenon she can be because she feels too comfortable where she is?

JT:

But we're at the point where we can do whatever we want to do.

Gary:

You could do whatever you want to do—but how are you going to change the world?

JT:

That is something I am really grateful for—we are in a position to be able to influence a change in the world.

Gary:

Yes, you are in the position to influence a change in the world. What are you doing to create that? How much money would you personally have to have, to willingly not take anything from VT and to make whatever you'd like to have happen in the world occur?

JT:

I think we contribute.

Gary:

I didn't ask about what you do together. How much money would you have to have in your own coffers to be able to throw away, waste, or burn, to create the change you would like to see in the world?

JT:

That would be billions, because it would be influencing the mining industry.

Gary:

So why aren't you creating that?

JT:

Well, I have started.

Gary:

You have the ability to create money. You like money. In fact, you love money. And you love your husband because he is willing to have money. People have tried to make you not have money or to make you believe that you couldn't have money on your own or that something about money was not your parlance, not your way of communicating. It's not true. And you won't step up to the brilliance of you until you are willing to receive from VT the money or the ways he gets money. You can learn from the man.

You've also got to be willing to recognize what you can take from VT. I want you to see his business acumen as a source of money and a force of money. You haven't been aggressive enough in taking the gifts he has available to you that could make you the millions and billions of dollars you want to make. You are willing to let him do it.

JT:

Yeah, he just kind of pulls money out of the air.

Gary:

He doesn't care where it comes from as long as it keeps coming. He likes money as much as you do, but you don't like creating as much as he does. What if you were willing to use him for whatever he could do to help you create? You feel that if you take his time or his energy or his awareness, that it's somehow taking money from him.

For him, creation is just one of the many ways he can have money. I am not sure exactly what it is for you. The best thing I can come up with is that you think his time equals his money. It doesn't. It's something along that line, because you won't take up his time to get him to teach you, to help you become the phenomenon with money you could be. And this applies to many of you here.

All of you who refuse to have the phenomenal capacity and the phenomenance of money, will you destroy and uncreate it all? Right and Wrong, Good and Bad, POD and POC, All 9, Shorts, Boys, and Beyonds.

What have you made so vital about never possessing the phenomenance of creating money that keeps you from dominating the world?

JT:

Not wanting to upset anybody.

Gary:

If you want to change the world, you've got to be willing to upset frigging anybody. That's what VT has. He has the ability to upset anybody. He doesn't care. You say, "I don't want to upset the applecart." Well, the only way you are going to get apple sauce is by upsetting the applecart. What have you made so vital about never possessing the phenomenance of creating money that keeps you from dominating the world?

Ladies, you've got to get this. I know you think you are quiet, mousey people. But you are actually dominatrices in hiding. You're hiding, yes. You don't wear the boots and the short shorts—but you would like to dominate the world.

The only way you are going to get apple sauce is
by upsetting the applecart.

IS WHATEVER YOU CREATE ENOUGH?

JT:

VT and I were talking about the difference between being contented and being really happy and creating. It goes back to what you were saying about changing the world.

Gary:

Yes, you have to create in order to have the happiness you want. Let's say you have a farm and you create a fabulous house on the farm, and it's all working and you say, "Okay, it's good." Are you still creating? Not necessarily. You've got to be creating it. Just adding some different animals is not creating it.

Is whatever you create enough? No, because you are an infinite being. The whole idea is that if you are truly being you, you have all choices available to you. If you are functioning from the *do, do, do* of it all, you have to figure out what you have to do in order to figure out whether that's creating something. But when you are actually being *you,* the creation of thousands of things is more interesting and real than two or ten. When you start to create from that place, everything else starts to work.

JT:

In the last month, we've had this contentment because we got the house paid off. Then just before we came here, I got really agitated. I was asking, "Is this it? We are content, we're so happy—but we're not."

Gary:

But you are. It's "We're content and we're happy *and* what else can we create?" You have to get that part. What if you were content and happy with everything you were creating all the time? You can try to make yourself content with a house, you can try to make yourself content with where you're living, but that is attempting to make that enough for you—and nothing will ever be enough for you because you are a humanoid.

When you are actually being you, the creation of thousands of things is more interesting and real than two or ten.

CREATING BEYOND THE LIMITATION

I recently got a notification from the IRS that I owed a huge amount of money. The same day, I went out and I bought something to put in the Antique Guild. Someone asked me, "How can you buy something like that when you owe so much money?"

I said, "I just owe money. I'm not dead. I'm still creating my life." How many of you stop your life based on what you owe?

Everything that is times a godzillion, will you destroy and uncreate it all? Right and Wrong, Good and Bad, POD and POC, All 9, Shorts, Boys, and Beyonds.

The only way you are going to get over owing something is to create all the time. You've got to create beyond the limitation of what you owe and then the money will start to happen fast. I started doing that and money started to come in faster and bigger and better. I wasn't willing to cut off my purchases or my creation based on the money I owed.

How many of you have stopped creating based on the fact that you owe someone or something? It's like "I owe my loyalty to my wife. I owe my life to my family. I owe my family for taking me in and keeping me part of the business." Everything you have done to make that your reality, will you destroy and uncreate it all? Right and Wrong, Good and Bad, POD and POC, All 9, Shorts, Boys, and Beyonds.

A lot of you do "I owe" to motivate yourself to create beyond it. What have you made so vital about owing that motivates you to get busy with mowing the lawn? Everything that is times a godzillion, will you destroy and uncreate it all? Right and Wrong, Good and Bad, POD and POC, All 9, Shorts, Boys, and Beyonds.

You're doing "I owe, so I go to work. I owe, so I've got to do it." What about asking: "What would I like to create in life?" What have you made so vital about never possessing the phenomenance of creation? Everything that is times a godzillion, will you destroy and uncreate it all? Right and Wrong, Good and Bad, POD and POC, All 9, Shorts, Boys, and Beyonds.

What have you made so vital about never possessing the phenomenance of creation that keeps you from doing the things you want to do? Everything that is times a godzillion, will you destroy and uncreate it all? Right and Wrong, Good and Bad, POD and POC, All 9, Shorts, Boys, and Beyonds.

You have to get that you have a choice. What choice would you like to make? What choice are you not making? What have you made so vital about never possessing the phenomenance of creation that keeps you in the limitation you are choosing? I keep changing the process because each time I say it something new comes up. Everything that is times a godzillion, will you destroy and uncreate it all? Right and Wrong, Good and Bad, POD and POC, All 9, Shorts, Boys, and Beyonds.

What have you made so vital about never possessing the phenomenance of creation that keeps you in limitation? Everything that is times a godzillion, will you destroy and uncreate it all? Right and Wrong, Good and Bad, POD and POC, All 9, Shorts, Boys, and Beyonds.

What have you made so vital about owing that motivates you to get busy with mowing the lawn?

THE BEAUTY OR THE BARGAIN?

LM:

Is that allowing money to control you?

Gary:

Yes, it's assuming that money is the criterion for what you can do. Many years ago I had lots of friends who dressed well by going to thrift stores and spending hours looking through racks of crappy stuff to find the one good thing that was in store. Or they would go to garage sales. I had one friend who would go to garage sales and there'd be a nice dress for $2.50 hanging on the fence with the tags on it from just having been dry-cleaned. She wouldn't buy it. She would go to a different garage sale and buy ten crappy dresses for twenty-five cents each. I kept asking, "Why are you doing this? This dress is perfect. It's in pristine condition and it would fit you." She'd say, "Yeah, but this is a better deal." She was more interested in the bargain than in the beauty.

I like bargains. Don't take the point of view that I don't like bargains. But people who go for the bargain always have to sell at a bargain price. People who get a good value on the beauty they buy always create more because the beauty is creative.

ND:

So when we're not aggressively seeking consciousness and creating our lives, are we doing the bargain basement thing?

Gary:

Yes. You're looking for the cheap gig.

ND:

There are two different energies, right?

Gary:

If you look for that which is a bargain based on its beauty instead of that which is a bargain based on its cheap price, you won't end up with a lot of cheap stuff in your life. You'll end up with a lot of beautiful stuff. And when you go to sell it, you can get more for it, based on its beauty, not its bargain capacity.

People who get a good value on the beauty they buy always create more because the beauty is creative.

CREATING THE PHENOMENANCE OF FUTURE

PR:

Is the phenomenance of creation realizing that everything is about creating something beyond the limitations of this reality, and then anything becomes possible? Most people try to create within the structure of this reality.

Gary:

The phenomenance of creation is knowing that what gets created today is going to create something tomorrow. What's it going to create? What's it going to look like? What am I going to have to deliver when it shows up? That is the phenomenance of creation. You never look for just handling now. You look at how to handle everything now *and* in the future.

PR:

So are you talking about being aware of the future in all the things you just said, and for you, that's undefinable as well?

Gary:

I don't try to define it. Most people try to define what they are going to need to determine, what they are going to decide, and what they are going to deliver. I ask:

+ What has to be here to fulfill the needs in the future?
+ What am I going to have to have here?

People look to the future from the point of view of "In the future, I will have this" or "This will occur." "I will have" or "This will occur" is not a phenomenal future in which everything changes. It may be an extraordinary future in which you get what you want the way you want it. What's beyond that is when you are willing to create a phenomenal future where bizarre and odd things occur. No, they don't actually *occur*. You *create* them. You create something that will create a different possibility in your life that you hadn't considered.

What have you made so vital about never possessing the phenomenance of future that you truly could create? Most of you don't think that you could have a phenomenal future. You think you can have a better future, a less stressful future, a future in which you'll have more money, but not a future that is so phenomenal that it changes everybody else's future. You are not willing to be the changeling that creates another future. Everything that is times a godzillion, will you destroy

and uncreate it all? Right and Wrong, Good and Bad, POD and POC, All 9, Shorts, Boys, and Beyonds.

What have you made so vital about never possessing the phenomenance of future are you choosing? Everything that is times a godzillion, will you destroy and uncreate it all? Right and Wrong, Good and Bad, POD and POC, All 9, Shorts, Boys, and Beyonds.

If you were willing to create something that no one else had ever seen before, what would you be creating? *That's* phenomenance. And you've got to be willing to look at what you have available as the phenomenance that will change everybody else's reality. I always do.

The future is created in each choice you make. The whispers of the future that will be are the strongest element of possibility that exists at the moment of your choice. They will speak to you if you are willing to hear them. It's a choice you have to make. Then you don't try to control the future nor do you try to make it go in the direction it's going to go. You simply ask the question, "What future is available here that I have not yet considered?"

The phenomenance of future would be not expecting it to look any particular way and knowing it could be better than you can possibly imagine. "How does it get any better than this?" That stupid-ass question I have been asking from the very beginning!

What have you made so vital about never possessing the phenomenance of future you could be choosing? Everything that is times a godzillion, will you destroy

and uncreate it all? Right and Wrong, Good and Bad, POD and POC, All 9, Shorts, Boys, and Beyonds.

The future is created in each choice you make.
If you were willing to create something that no one else
had ever seen before, what would you be creating?
That's phenomenance.

Being and Doing

BEING UNDEFINED AND UNDEFINABLE

Gary:

In 1970 I saved my money and went to Europe for six months. I bought a car, and at that time you could go to the American Express office in a city and somebody would be holding a sign that said, "Going to such-and-such a place. Will pay for gas." I would pick up somebody and I would travel with them for three weeks and then I would travel with someone else. I kept doing that as I made my way through Europe. It was a great adventure, and I got to create myself anew every day, because there was no one who could define who I was, or where I was, or what I was to them.

AN:

The most fun I ever had was when I was in Venice by myself for four days. I didn't have any thoughts or visions of what I was doing or where I was going or how I needed to show up. I always have the most fun when I do that.

Gary:

So that's really you. That's your reality.

AN:

Yeah, that's fun for me. But I see that I keep trying to get back into this reality.

Gary:

Try asking: "If I was choosing my reality, what would I do or be here?"

AN:

It would be completely undefined.

Gary:

Yes, and if you have an undefined reality, you cannot be confined by anyone or anything else.

AN:

And it doesn't require any defense, ever.

Gary:

Nope. You never have to defend anything. You only have to choose everything.

AN:

Is there something about this I'm not getting?

Gary:

Yes, stop trying to define things.

What if you were no longer definable by your own reality? Everything that is times a godzillion, will you destroy and uncreate it all? Right and Wrong, Good and Bad, POD and POC, All 9, Shorts, Boys, and Beyonds.

If you have an undefined reality, you cannot
be confined by anything or anyone else.

Stop trying to do a vision board or you're going to be bored with your life. If you had no vision of who you were, who would you be?

ES:

I would go to awareness. I am cutting off awareness with all of the ways I am defining myself as "I am." I realize how often I go to an "I am." "I am happy" or "I am wonderful" or "I am fabulous" as a way to resist or get away from the ugly, mean, penurious, and contracted.

Gary:

You just stated it. Going to "I am" is trying to get away *from* something; it's not going *to* something. What could you go to if you were functioning from "What are the infinite possibilities?" Any time you do "I am," you are defining yourself. You are cutting off your awareness of what can actually be. That's the reason for the four questions:

- What is this?
- What do I do with it?
- Can I change it?
- And if so, how do I change it?

Those four questions are designed to get you out of the "I am" universe.

JT:

I get that I am putting a limitation on myself when I say, "I am." So what do I say when people want to know what I do? I struggle to find the words.

Gary:

Don't worry about it. Don't make it real for you. You can say, "I'm an entrepreneur. I'm a fashion model. I'm a superior being. I'm a wonderful person and you don't get to touch me."

What could you go to if you were functioning from "What are the infinite possibilities?" instead of "I am"?

WHEN YOU ARE BEING, YOU CAN DO ANYTHING

CB:

I have a resistance about *doing*.

Gary:

Why would you be resistant to doing? Why do you choose resistance to doing as a valuable product to you? Why would *doing* ever be a problem?

CB:

That is what I am thinking too. Is it that *doing* is a problem when I am not *being*?

Gary:

When you are *being*, you can do anything. *Doing* just proves you are being. When you stop being able to *do*, you stop *being*. If you are resisting doing something, it is because you are resisting being something. So when you find yourself resistant to doing something, ask: "What am I resisting being here that would create a greater possibility and a greater reality?"

CB:

So *being* is the energy of *easily doing?*

Gary:

Yes, ease of doing is based on the ease of being. The more you are willing to *be*, the more you can *do* with no point of view. In this reality, you learn to do in order to prove you are being something. If I do law, that proves I am being a lawyer and I am being a better person.

When you are truly being everything, you can do anything. And you have no point of view about doing it. "Oh, I would like to do that. I'd like to do that. I'll do that. I'll do that. I'll do that." It is just choice. People ask me, "How do you do all of the stuff you do?"

I say, "By choice."

They ask, "What do you mean?"

I say, "How do I do it? I just do it."

CB:

Do I need to POD and POC proving that I need to do?

Gary:

No, POD and POC everything that you are not *being*, because if you have to prove something, there's something you are not being. This is all the *being* stuff. Being is so frigging important and it is ignored. No church, cult, or religion besides Access asks you to *be*. They ask you to *do*, they ask you to *prove*, they ask you to do all kinds of stuff except *be*.

Ease of doing is based on the ease of being.

GOING DOWN THE "DOING" TRACK

NK:

Could you expand on the idea of being, doing, necessity, and creation? I always tend to go down the "doing" track. I do what I "have" to do.

Gary:

You were taught that you have to *do* in order to prove something.

NK:

That was the valuable thing. The valuable product was a doing.

Gary:

And the only thing valuable about you was what you could do for others to prove that you loved them enough. How did that work for you?

NK:

Not at all.

Gary:

So why do you keep choosing it?

NK:

Some sort of stupidity plus autopilot.

Gary:

You are not willing to create your reality. But you've made a mistake. You married somebody who will always create her reality and who will beat the shit out of you if you don't choose yours.

HB:

The other day NK was complaining about money, as usual. At first I started to go down the route of asking him questions and facilitating him. Then I said, "Wait a minute, he works ten to thirteen hours a day and he makes less money than anybody I know who works that hard. That is a talent. This man works all the time." I don't even know how anyone could work so hard and make such a small amount of money. I don't know how that's possible.

Gary:

You could just look at him and say, "Cuckoo. Cuckoo. Cuckoo." The good part about this is that he's not embarrassed. He is smiling.

NK:

It is a frigging joke, really.

Gary:

No, it's not a joke! It makes you happy to work for no money.

How many of you have made yourselves happy to work for nothing? That is even worse than I thought it was going to be. Everything that is times a godzillion, will you destroy and uncreate it all? Right and Wrong, Good and Bad, POD and POC, All 9, Shorts, Boys, and Beyonds.

NK:

I see that it always comes down to receiving and valuing myself.

Gary:

No, it is not about receiving.

NK:

It's not about receiving? My not having money is not about receiving?

Gary:

No.

NK:

What is it about?

Gary:

What is the one thing you won't give that would get you money? You will give of yourself, you will give of your time. What won't you give of?

NK:

I have no idea. What won't I give of?

Gary:

I think you need to keep asking the question until you become aware of it.

ST:

I want to know!

Gary:

Enquiring minds always want to know.

ST:

Hurry up, NK, come on!

NK:

Tune in tomorrow.

Gary:

Ask: "What am I not willing to give of?"

NK:

My being. Of me. All of me.

Gary:

Yes, you won't give all of you. You'll *do* until the cows come home but you won't give any of you.

NK:

What is giving of me?

Gary:

Giving of you is the willingness to be the phenomenance of you—regardless of anybody else's point of view. How often do you determine what you do based on somebody else's point of view?

NK:

All the time.

Gary:

You obviously want to step up or you wouldn't have created a relationship with a woman who is as demanding as HB.

NK:

I am very aware of that.

Gary:

What would it take for you to give you in totality?

NK:

So it is being the phenomenance of me, no matter what anybody else's point of view is?

Gary:

Yes, you always adjust yourself for other people's point of view. You should read *Divorceless Relationship*. Actually, you should make it your bible. You keep divorcing yourself, thinking you are creating a greater relationship, but all you do is create less of you in the world, with more doing and less money.

That is why you can't have money. If you were giving of you, then you would say, "Wait a minute, I'm not valuing me. I will have more money." If you just do what other people require of you and you give up your point of view, you can justify that you don't need to get any money for what you did, because you are not giving anything of yourself.

NK:

So, it is a commitment to the phenomenance of being? Am I trying to make this too solid or too tangible?

Gary:

You are trying to define phenomenance of being by the reality you have already decided is so instead of choosing a reality beyond this reality that is actually yours. This is where you have to choose to be the phenomenance you are. I am working on all of this phenomenance stuff because I'm hoping at some point that all of you can get that you will be phenomenal with everything. What you have been phenomenal with so far is limitation, lies, judgment, control, feelings, thoughts, emotions, and pathetic victimhood. What about the *greatness* of you?

There is the phenomenance of you, the phenomenance of your body, and the phenomenance of embodiment. Embodiment is this whole reality. It's not just the body. Once you function from the phenomenance of embodiment, you begin to see the greatness that is all around us. It's quite dynamic.

Giving of you is the willingness to be the phenomenance of you—regardless of anybody else's point of view.

269

CHOOSE TO NEVER DIMINISH YOUR AWARENESS

NM:

Can you talk about being expanded when we are doing something?

Gary:

Many of you seem to think that if you focus on something, you will have more awareness of it, but that is not true. Less focus actually equals more awareness. The less you focus, the more awareness you have available to complete any task. All tasks can be completed without focus.

NM:

Is it about being expanded?

Gary:

No, it is choosing to never diminish your awareness. I watch people do this all the time. When FB is at the Antique Guild, he expands his awareness continuously. He has an awareness of all of the rooms, even the ones he is not in. He always recognizes the energy of somebody who is about to be interested in something and he just happens to join that person in the space they are in. But in the other areas of his life, he contracts his awareness to fit other people's reality.

FB:

It's like when you walk into a room and you know that someone is horny or that sex is available in their universe.

Gary:

Yes, but why aren't you living that every day and every moment of your life?

FB:

Well, I am always in the Guild, so that is actually most of my life.

Gary:

Nice justification, dude.

FB:

Where am I not being the expansion I am being when I am at the Guild?

Gary:

When you walk, you don't keep an expanded space. You diminish your awareness to the surrounds of your body. You move your *body* through space; *you* don't move through space.

FB:

If my body is moving through space, then where am I?

Gary:

That is what I want to know.

FB:

Me too.

MOVING *WITH* YOUR BODY

Gary:

Most of you contract your energy to make the body move rather than moving the body with you through space.

Years ago somebody said to me, "I recognized you three blocks away. I could tell by the way you walked that it was you. You walk different than other people do." At first I didn't understand what she meant, but I finally realized that I walk *with my body* through space. I don't walk my body through space. It is not something I *intend* to do. It is something I *am doing.* When you intend to walk your body through space, you put your intention on contracting everything enough to figure out where you are going to put your body, as though if you don't, you will fall down or bump into something.

FB:

That is how I drive as well. I get that it is a limitation, but it takes a lot of effort to do it differently.

Gary:

It shouldn't take effort. It should be that you're aware of where you are in the scheme of walking your body.

FB:

I have made that boring, so I am somewhere else, doing something else.

Gary:

Yeah, you use the least amount of energy you can to be with your body rather than being the expanded space of possibility. That is something your body is capable of too.

FB:

Have you always noticed that with me?

Gary:

Yes. You tend to walk your body through space rather than being the space you are with your body. Be in that same sense of space of being with your body, not just walking it through space.

FB:

It is like I have made my body a foreign instrument. And then if you add a car on top of that, it's a lot to manipulate with the body that I already feel is kind of weird. I could never play the piano.

Gary:

That is because you never do it from your space of *being*. You do it from the space of functioning with this weird instrument called a body. And the only part you saw any advantage to having was butt muscles and a penis.

FB:

And a voice.

Gary:

When you sing people say, "Oh my God!"

FB:

Those are the times when there isn't a barrier between the energy that I am and what I know is possible. There is just no barrier.

Gary:

That's correct. There is no barrier to being everything you actually are. And if you function with your body and your car and everything else with no barrier to being everything you are, everything is greater and better and easier.

FB:

Okay, I am grappling for a way to do that.

Gary:

Well, it is not a grapple; it is a practice. You know how to play with the body parts you like. What if you started liking the body parts you haven't played with yet?

FB:

As if they were antiques?

Gary:

Yes.

FB:

Thank you. I have never been aware of that until now. How do I take the areas where I am being the expanded space of possibility and permeate it out into everything?

Gary:

What if you could be a worldwide authority and a worldwide source for all of the antiques and jewels that are worth having?

FB:

I realized that I don't do that from judgment, and so many people do. They're always judging what is valuable and what is not.

Gary:

Other people do it from conclusion and judgment, and you do it from "Oh! What is this?" You do it from the questions:

+ What is this and how can this be fun?
+ How can we use this?
+ What would we use this for?

GG:

I've noticed that when we are working with people and with bodies, we forget to choose us. And when we are using our bodies and we are exercising and forcing ourselves to do things, we do the same thing. What would happen if we were the invitation to our bodies to come and play, so when we go out for a walk we actually go for a *walk with our body* rather than taking *our body for a walk?*

Gary:

That is what I am talking about. You treat your body like a dog that is on a leash. You don't treat it like it is something you are having fun with.

GG:

If you go down to the mall, you see people who look like zombies. They're taking their bodies for a walk. You'll also see others who are walking *with* their bodies and it is like "¡Ay, caramba!" There is such a difference. Watch them. They are so in their bodies and so sexual with their bodies. They stand upright and the others walk around with their hands and knuckles dragging on the ground.

If you function with your body and your car and
everything else with no barrier to being everything you
are, everything is greater and better and easier.

THE SPACE OF BEING

DW:

In talking about being expanded and not diminishing our awareness, do the questions "What am I being? Where am I being? How am I being? When am I being?" allow us to be more of that space of being?

Gary:

Yes, because there are places in your life, as FB said, where you will be that. But you will not *always* be that.

MP, you will be that expanded space, then you will contract your energy in order to figure out how to put down your cup and your microphone, because you somehow don't feel like you are connected to all of that. You should be doing those things within the structure of *being,* not through the structure of your *body.* I get results with horses that other people don't get because I function through being, not doing. I don't function with my body as something that I have to stand outside and manipulate, but so many people do.

DW:

Is there anything more that I need to be aware of?

Gary:

All I can do is tell you about this. I can show you the energy of it but I don't know how to tell you what to do. I can say that I see you not choosing it. Maybe something else would show up if you tried it and played with it and practiced it.

I function through being, not doing.
I don't function with my body as something that I have to stand outside and manipulate, but so many people do.

You and Your Body

VULNERABILITY WITH YOUR BODY

GR:

Could you talk about vulnerability with your body?

Gary:

Vulnerability with your body is not putting up barriers to it or making it do things it can't do or doesn't want to do. It's asking, "Body, do you want this?"

I went to lunch today. It was a buffet. I said, "Body, we need some vegetables."

My body said, "No."

I asked, "What do you mean, 'No'?"

My body said, "No."

"But we need vegetables."

"No."

"Okay, what do you want? That?"

"No."

"That?"

"No"

"That?"

"No. What's that over there?"

It was ham. My body wanted ham. I ate four pieces of ham. I haven't eaten four pieces of meat in six months. One little piece is enough usually. I was stuffing ham in. The waitress came and ripped my plate out from under me. I said, "But I'm not done yet!" I wanted to go back for more.

Vulnerability with your body is the place where you allow your body to tell you what it wants and what it doesn't. It's listening to your body in such a way that you have no judgment of it, you don't try to control it, and you don't tell it what's good.

This morning SM said, "I've got a headache." I said, "Your body needs something. What does your body need that you are not ingesting?"

He said, "Fruit."

I happened to have a banana in my hand, and his body said, "Mine!"

I said, "Your body definitely needs some fruit."

He said, "Let's see if they have any bananas downstairs."

ST looked at him and said, "I think you need a Coke." He drank one Coke and started to feel better, then he drank another Coke and started to feel good, and with the third one he felt almost normal. That's because your body sugar is eaten up by these processes. Everybody tells you that sugar is bad for you, but your body needs way more sugar than we take in on this planet. Listen to your body, ask what it wants, and let it have that.

ARE YOU IN CONFLICT WITH YOUR BODY?

PA:

I am asking my body questions but I can't get a connection.

Gary:

Do you have any desire to be connected to your body?

PA:

Well, I perceive that I do.

Gary:

What have you decided your body is supposed to tell you that it is not telling you? Or what is it telling you that you are not receiving? That one. Is it telling you something you are not receiving? Or is it telling you something that you really don't want to hear?

PA:

That one.

Gary:

Everything you have done to not perceive, know, be, and receive what your body is actually telling you, will you destroy and uncreate it all? Right and Wrong, Good and Bad, POD and POC, All 9, Shorts, Boys, and Beyonds.

PA:

I'll override it.

Gary:

Well, that's a typical humanoid. Override your body and make it do what it doesn't want to do because that's way more fun for you.

PA:

Well, it's not.

Gary:

Are you sure?

PA:

It's not working for me.

Gary:

I know, because your body is really pissed now.

PA:

Yes, that's where it is. It's pissed.

Gary:

It's pissed. You're pissed at it, it's pissed at you, and the two of you have a great conflict going on. It's the Seven Years' War.

PA:

It feels like it, yes.

Gary:

What have you made so vital about not possessing a body that creates a constant state of conflict with your body?

PA:

I don't see a value in having a body.

Gary:

And your body says, "I don't see any value in having you, either." You won't get out and go away, and it can't kick you out. Why won't you go away?

PA:

I don't know.

Gary:

Are you sure it is not because you value life so much that you don't want to die?

PA:

That, yes. I value life, but I don't value living.

Gary:

You have got to practice living. I'm sorry. This is not one I can POD and POC. Practice living. Here's how you practice living: What kind of furniture do you sit on? Is it really comfortable? Can you cush into it and really enjoy it?

PA:

Yes.

Gary:

Okay, good. What kind of food do you eat?

PA:

I don't buy cheap food.

Gary:

I did not ask whether it was cheap.

PA:

Nice food.

Gary:

Nice. What the heck does "nice food" mean?

PA:

It tastes good.

Gary:

It tastes good. Is it what your body wants? No. You don't eat for your body, do you?

PA:

No. That would have to be a *no*.

Gary:

Okay, so you have got to start asking: "Body, what do you want to eat?" and even if it's cheap and ugly, eat it.

PA:

Okay.

Gary:

What do you drink?

PA:

Red wine.

Gary:

Does your body like red wine or does it like a different kind of wine?

PA:

It likes red wine.

Gary:

Okay, and how much of it do you drink?

PA:

I have a couple of glasses.

Gary:

Does it want more than that?

PA:

No, I don't think so.

Gary:

What else does it like to drink?

PA:

Water.

Gary:

Really? Or do *you* like to drink water?

PA:

I like to drink water.

Gary:

I think your body wants to drink something other than water or wine.

PA:

Can you give me a clue? Or do I have to ask my body?

Gary:

You might want to ask your body, but I get your body is saying, "How about some beer, damn it?"

PA:

I hate beer.

Gary:

I know, but your body doesn't.

PA:

Right, okay.

Gary:

Try a Monteith's Black.

PA:

Ew, okay.

Gary:

Have you drunk that before?

PA:

I have, actually. But only a small portion. I couldn't drink it. It was too revolting.

Gary:

Yep, conflict with your body. "Body, what do you want to drink?" I wish they had James Squire Amber Ale over here.

Dain:

That would be awesome. My question is: Does your body like to ride motorcycles really fast and ride jet skis and jump over waves and run out and be naked and lie in the sun? Oh right, probably not, okay, bye.

Gary:

Dain, was that your body trying to inspire PA's body? PA, you've got to give your body things that give it a sense of joy.

PA:

I feel that because I'm not doing that, I am not doing the creative, generative part of myself well.

Gary:

If you are in a constant state of conflict with your body, does your body contribute to your making it easier to deliver what you can?

PA:

No, it doesn't.

Gary:

You have to start doing what would be fun for your body. What kind of movement would your body actually like?

PA:

Um...

Gary:

Okay, that's "No bloody clue."

PA:

Swimming, actually.

Gary:

And you have been doing a lot of that, right?

PA:

No, I haven't. I have been avoiding it.

Gary:

Well, that's a good idea! That way you will make your body suffer. Then your body will make you suffer, and then what we have is a suffering duet. Your body likes to move, and you are not moving it. You've got to start moving it. You're acting like it is some kind of feeble, old lady body. It doesn't *want* to be a feeble, old lady body. If you are going to do something, make sure it is fun for your body. You don't have fun with your body, and therefore, your body won't let you have fun in life.

PA:

Thank you.

You have to start doing what would be fun for your body. What kind of movement would your body actually like?

PHYSICAL DISABILITY AND VICTIMHOOD

DJ:

As a result of an accident, I've been in a wheelchair since I was sixteen years old. A few years ago I was fed up with my limitations and I was talking about leaving the planet. You gave me a gift when you said, "You want to leave? Okay, make a list of what you would like to create in another body." I had a sense that maybe this was a conclusion for me, but then I said, "I think I have to stay and change whatever is going on in this body." Have I created the victim thing?

Gary:

No, you don't do victim for shit.

DJ:

I didn't think so.

Gary:

You are always pushing people away so they can't help you … and at the same time you're saying, "Help me." You're really mean. You say, "Help me. No, I'm fine."

DJ:

What do I have to do to change that?

Gary:

Why don't you ask: "How mean can I be with the mean machine I've created as me?" Be careful, that's kind of appealing to you.

DJ:

Yes, it is in a way. What does that bring to the world?

Gary:

Most people consider that everybody who has a disability is incredibly nice and kind because they seem to need people so much. The idea is that if you need people a lot, you will be a better person.

DJ:

It pisses me off that my disability attracts people who want to help.

Gary:

Yeah, it attracts people who have a lot of superiority. They are not interested in actually contributing to you. They are interested in proving how cool they are that they "helped" you.

DJ:

I resist that a lot.

Gary:

I know. It's appropriate to resist it, because they are doing superior when they "help" you. They are not doing contribution. When somebody is a true contribution to you, you receive it dynamically. When we do body processes and people put you on a table to work on you, I have watched the difference between the ones who are willing to contribute to you and to work with you, and those who are thinking, "I'll help the poor crippled guy." That's what victims are looking for—someone who wants to help the poor crippled guy or girl. That's why you're not a victim.

DJ:

I have had some magical healing stuff show up with people I've worked on lately and I am starting to get that I can be a contribution to the world.

Gary:

How many people do you know who go to doctors, nurses, and practitioners and get no result?

DJ:

A lot.

Gary:

And how many people do you know who don't look for a different possibility for themselves or others? A lot. There are many people out there who wish there was something else, and they don't know where to go or how to get it. A lot of them are committing suicide or making their body shut down because there is no joy in living without an awareness that contribution can be gifted without an exchange, without a token, without a need to prove that somehow the person making the contribution is better for having given to you.

Lots of people have contributed to you and been magnificent in their contribution. That's a rare gift. That's one of the things allowance teaches—the willingness to gift without the necessity of proving anything. I love the people in Access. The allowance that comes with them blows me away. Again and again people send me texts or emails that say, "The tools of Access have saved my life. The tools of Access allowed me to do this for this friend. The tools of Access allowed this to happen." That's what makes my life worth living.

I'll stick around a long time, just because I keep getting accolades for how the tools and the people of Access are contributing to a better world. I don't mean *better* in the sense that the world is a kinder, gentler place. I mean *better* in the sense that there is no judgment of what people choose. There is an awareness that people can have a different possibility. That, to me, is the greatest gift there is.

DJ:

The reason I have stuck around is that I have a sense of something I can bring to the world but I am not sure what that is.

Gary:

It's *you.* You should be on television. What could you change in people's perspective by your awareness in this body? If you spoke up, if you wrote a book, if you did a telecall, you could ask: "When disability is considered your only choice, where do you go?"

DJ:

I have to make this body walk first.

Gary:

No, you can go faster on wheels. I learned that long ago. I've been outrun by people on wheels.

DJ:

Thank you.

LM:

Could DJ ask, "What advantage could this physical disability be to me?"

Gary:

Well, it gets him money, it gets him sympathy.

LM:

Would that be a good process?

Gary:

Are you doing that for DJ or for you?

LM:

For DJ.

Gary:

Stop trying to help him. He will punch you out if you are not careful!

What could you change in people's perspective
by your awareness in this body?

DEATH AND DYING

I received a bunch of texts this morning from a woman who is helping to caretake the ranch of a lady who is dying. She said, "I hate that the lady won't eat."

I said, "That's an indication that her body wants to die. Just let her not eat." They are forcing her to eat to keep her alive when she is dying, which is insane. When the body gets to the point where it doesn't want to eat, that is because it doesn't want to live anymore. The body will not eat if it doesn't want to live. If you force it to eat to keep it alive, who are you being kind to?

The woman said, "I hate the fact that she is alone so much."

The lady is taking all kinds of drugs, and they knock her out so she stays in bed for five or six hours alone. I said, "Be happy she is alone. That makes it easier on the being."

Drugs may put the person out but they don't take away the suffering. When people are in pain, they get drug cocktails that are supposed to take away the pain, but they only black the person out so they can't "experience" the pain. The body still has it. The drugs only take away the appearance of pain. The body still suffers. Exit Stage Left is the best thing that you can do for anybody who is dying.

Later the woman who is doing the caretaking sent me a text that said, "The lady is at her desk today. She is upright and at her desk." Granted she couldn't walk there, granted they had to hold her there, granted they had to feed her while she was sitting at her computer, but "she went to her desk" as though that's a gift.

I said, "She went to her desk to try and finish up the things she hasn't done because she realizes death is coming." Most people resist death by not completing things. The things they haven't completed are the things you have to take care of when they die. You have to know that and set everything up so it can be taken care of easily. I am having this conversation with you because I want you to get that there is a place where death begins because the person is done. They are done; that's all it is.

WHEN PEOPLE STICK AROUND AFTER THEY DIE

Oftentimes people stay in a particular location after they die because they are confused. It often happens with people who die in accidents. Sometimes when there is an accident involving somebody who was drinking heavily or doing drugs, you will see them on the side of the road trying to stop people, because they think they can get saved. Have you ever been in certain areas of a city where traffic slows down all of a sudden for no apparent reason? You can run: "Dissipate and release all of the drugs and everything that is trying to keep a person stuck here." The only place it doesn't work is where there are indigenous people on land they believe got stolen from them.

DW:

What do you do then?

Gary:

I have tried several times and I could get them to go away for a few weeks and the traffic would flow through that area magnificently and then all of a sudden it would start backing up again. I realized they were out there screaming, "This is my land. You can't cross it!" It is their land and they don't want you driving over it.

I am giving you this information because a lot of you have people in your lives who are going to start dying. Why? Because the Earth is changing. When there are major changes on the Earth, as there are now, lots of people choose to leave because they can't handle the change. Be aware of this so you are prepared for what happens.

DJ:

You have said that people in native cultures often have a lot of beliefs and stick around after they die, and we have talked about the entities on our farm in New Zealand. Something is coming up in me about this. Is there something that needs to change in the beliefs that hold all of these entities there?

Gary:

The Maoris don't believe they own the land. They believe they *belong to the land.* So when they die, they stick around because they belong to the land. It's "This is the land I belong to" not "This is the land I own." They have a greater sense of communion with the land than many other cultures. So if they are fighting for the land that they belong to, they stick there almost eternally. This belief eliminates their ability to leave with ease and makes it harder for them to choose a different reality.

People also tend to get stuck when they are buried in a site that is not acknowledged as a burial ground, for instance, in mass graves from battles or massacres that were covered up. The acknowledgment that the land is the site of a battle or a massacre is the only thing that gives them the potential for leaving.

DJ:

That is kind of uncomfortable for me. I feel as though I have a lot of stuff going on around this.

Gary:

There are a lot of Maoris that are a wrong package. Those are non-Maori people who committed massacres against the Maoris. They felt so bad and so guilty that they ended up coming back as a Maori to suffer at the hands of the Pakeha (white men) so they could prove that what they did to the Maoris was somehow all right. There are a lot of wrong package Maoris and Pakeha here in New Zealand. They are people who look white and are actually Maoris—like you. You look like a white guy and you have blue eyes but you are more black inside than you are white.

DJ:

I would like to get free of that.

Gary:

No, you don't want to get free of it; you need to learn how to use it. Manipulate it and use it. If you are willing to use it, you will ultimately get free of it, because it is no longer the reason for or against anything. As long as there is a reason for or against something, you stick yourself.

This also applies to entities. When you wish to set entities free, ask what they are fighting for and what they are working against. Then ask whether that is actually working for them or whether something else would be greater or easier.

As long as there is a reason for or against something, you stick yourself.

The Phenomenance of Your Sexual Reality

YOUR SEXUAL REALITY IS ABOUT HOW YOU RECEIVE

Gary:

When I talk about your sexual reality, some of you think I'm talking about having sex. No. I'm not talking about who you shag, what you shag, or when you shag. Your sexual reality is about *how you receive*. It is not about who you get to copulate with.

When you are being vulnerable, you never put up a barrier to anything. Vulnerability is asking, "What can I receive that other people are giving that they don't even know they are giving?" You can receive everything. That doesn't mean that you get stomped on. You guys think vulnerability equals being a doormat. No. It means that you can stomp somebody to death, because that is part of receiving too. Say someone is dismissing you and looking at you as not valuable. That's a great gift. I consider it a gift when people are cruel. I say, "Okay. Thanks, bye. I don't have to consider you anymore."

GR:

I will go and play with someone who is fun.

Gary:

Yes. What if your sexual reality is about "I'll go play"? Your sexual reality may be different than everybody else's. This doesn't make you wrong; it just makes you different. If you can get that for you, sex is not the same as it is for other people, you can create a relationship that will work for you.

You have to get what your sexual reality is or you cannot create a relationship that will work for you. You will only create a relationship that will work for the other person. We have a new body process called The Phenomenance of Your Sexual Reality, which is done in the Advanced Body Class. It may screw up a lot of your points of view because it begins to undo the places where you have *decided* what your sexual reality is and you begin to see what *it actually is*, which for some of you is not going to be comfortable. I was talking with someone who said, "If this person doesn't have sex with me, it is going to destroy my whole reality." In other words, "My whole reality and my whole universe are tied up in sex."

I said, "What?!" This explains a lot of the craziness that goes on in religions, where it is all about "Don't have sex, don't do sex, and don't be sexual." It makes no sense. These bodies were designed for having fun. Your body should be your toy. Do you do sex as play? Or do you do sex as if you were dealing with a major significance? When sex cannot be a toy, it cannot be a joy. And when it cannot be a joy, it cannot be your reality. You are confining you to the human reality which is the significance of it all.

What have you made so vital about never possessing the phenomenance of your sexual reality that keeps you stuck in human limitation? Everything that is times a godzillion, will you destroy and uncreate it all? Right and Wrong, Good and Bad, POD and POC, All 9, Shorts, Boys, and Beyonds.

You've got to find out what your sexual reality is. What have you made so vital about never possessing the phenomenance of your sexual reality that keeps you stuck in human limitation? Have you ever noticed that your sexual reality as a humanoid is different from what humans choose? In human reality, trauma and drama, upset and intrigue are connected to sex. Ever notice? It's never about the fun or the joy of it. It's always about the rightness or wrongness of it.

What if your sexual reality didn't include the rightness and wrongness of it? What if your sexual reality created the possibility of it? Different possibility, different reality, different everything. Everything that is times a godzillion, will you destroy and uncreate it all? Right and Wrong, Good and Bad, POD and POC, All 9, Shorts, Boys, and Beyonds.

You have to get what's real for you. Let's say that you're freer than other people, so you try to make that right—which is human reality. Or you make yourself wrong for being that free—which creates judgment, which creates a diminishment of your sexual possibilities. I believe that finding out what your sexual reality is will open you up to a whole different universe sexually.

If your sexual reality is "I never want to have it," that should be okay. But it is *not* okay, is it? In this reality, you're wrong for whatever your sexual reality is. You are wrong for not having it, you're wrong for having it, you're wrong for liking it, you're wrong for not liking it. Where does the freedom and the phenomenance of possibility begin? When you start to have your own sexual reality.

> *When sex cannot be a toy, it cannot be a joy.*
> *And when it cannot be a joy, it cannot be your reality.*

ND:

I have made myself wrong for so much of my life. I am so tired of making myself wrong that I have gone to making myself right.

Gary:

I am hoping this sexual reality process will get you to the place where you can see what your reality is in a whole lot of other areas, because sexual reality is the one place where there is a constant, never-ending, continually expanding judgment. And that shouldn't be. It should be:

- Okay, what can I do?
- Who do I want to do?

It should be a question always, but it's not. It's always a conclusion.

From my perspective, this is the beginning of you truly coming out of judgment of yourself. It may take a little while, and that's the reason you have to play with it or practice at it. You have to ask: "If I was choosing my reality, what would my sexual reality be?" You are an infinite being and there isn't anything or anyone you haven't done. Have you been a homosexual? Have you had sex with children? Yeah. Have you had sex with dead bodies? Have you done it with donkeys? Yeah. There is pretty much nothing you haven't tried at one time or another, but you go into judgment of that. I have said for years that sexuality is always a judgment. If you define yourself into your sexuality, it is always a judgment.

"If I was choosing my reality, what
would my sexual reality be?"

DEFINING YOURSELF INTO YOUR SEXUALITY

MP:

Is the question "What would my sexual reality *look like?*" or is it "What would my sexual reality *be?*"

Gary:

Be. Why do you guys go to *look like?* Do you want to stand outside yourself and watch yourself have sex? Or do you want to *be* something?

MP:

That's part of my question. One moment it would be this and the next moment it would be that. I get confused.

Gary:

You are trying to choose one or the other instead of realizing, "My sexual reality includes this *and* this." Let's say that your sexual reality included men and women. Would you be bisexual— or would you not have to label yourself?

MP:

I can see the possibility of having both where I wouldn't have to label myself. It would just be my sexual reality.

Gary:

All of you keep trying to define yourself, label yourself, and categorize yourself. In this reality, you are supposed to define what your sexuality is. It is about confining all of your choices. The only choice you are allowed to have is that you are straight, and if you are not straight, then you are gay. But that doesn't give you the place to be everything you are or to choose anything at any moment. Being willing and able to have total choice is the place we should live.

I had two female friends who had each been married and divorced. They ended up getting a house together because they couldn't afford a house by themselves anymore. They were having a great time as housemates and they adored each other. One day they got very drunk, fell into bed together, and decided they were lesbians. What question is "We are lesbians"? It's not a question! "Can I go down on you now?" would have been a question—but instead of asking that, they made a decision and defined themselves into sexuality. They decided they had to like it. And then they broke up. Within two years, each one of them was married to a man. So were they lesbians? No, they just enjoyed each other. What if you could have that as a reality without the necessity of defining yourself? You should have all possibility.

Not having your own sexual reality is what keeps the battle of the sexes in place. I did *Salon des Femmes* to give women a place to recognize what it actually means to be a woman. And I did *The Gentlemen's Club* to give men a place to recognize what it means to truly be a man and not have a judgment about the rightness or the wrongness of their sex, but to have the joy and the possibility that it could create.

I am hoping this will be the beginning of a change that will allow for a different kind of relationship and a different kind of sexual reality on Earth. I have always known it was possible, but until we got to this phenomenance thing, I didn't know what to do with it.

Being willing and able to have total
choice is the place we should live.

TOTAL RECEIVING

TS:

When you talk about our sexual reality, what comes up for me is how many of the men I have slept with wanted something for *them* rather than something for *me*.

Gary:

That's the way you've been trying to get your sexual reality. You've looked for what you can give to others—but that's not your sexual reality. That's trying to prove to yourself that you have a sexual reality. It doesn't give you the space of actually seeing what your sexual reality might be. What if your sexual reality was not just men or just women but the sexual energy of every moment of every day? Orgasmic living is closer to what true sexualness is than anything else. You should be able to eat a person the way you eat a great meal. Totally enjoying every flavor and every taste you get.

TS:

Total receiving.

Gary:

Most people in this reality do not use sex as receiving. For them, sex is not receiving. It is doing and delivering. It is not the wholesomeness of phenomenal gifting and receiving simultaneously.

TS:

That is really a totally different reality.

Gary:

That's my reality.

TS:

My not having my sexual reality and instead having sex for other people, how would that play out in my whole reality?

Gary:

You begin to think your universe is dedicated to doing for others. Unfortunately, because of the sexual conditioning of human reality, sex is about what you are supposed to do. You are supposed to have kids, you are supposed to do this, you are supposed to do that. It is all of the *supposed to's* that determine what is wrong with you when you don't do them.

TS:

Whenever someone needs something, sexually or otherwise, I go into "I am here. I'm delivering." There's not even a question.

Gary:

There is no question and there is no place for you to determine what would work for you. You pretty much lose the Kingdom of We in favor of the Kingdom of Me in every sexual encounter you have.

TS:

That happens in any kind of encounter. It is not just in bed.

Gary:

Yes. This is why I am hoping you will get that the phenomenance of having your own sexual reality means you can choose more. It opens the door to choice. Right now you have the choice locked in place with "This is my universe with regard to sex."

TS:

It's like a different box. It's as if I'm saying, "This is the department of sex."

Gary:

This is the department of sex and you've reached your quota. You're not allowed to have any more sex. "What? How did I reach my quota? I haven't even done that much. All that masturbation? All that practice I had."

At one point I was on a television show in New Zealand, and I talked about teaching your kid to masturbate so he would be a better lover. I said, "Teach him to do it slow and easy and enjoy it, and he will be a better lover." The guy who was interviewing me was thrilled. He said, "I am going to go home and teach my kid how to masturbate. He's ten. Is that too early?"

I said, "Not as long as you teach him how to do it slow and easy instead of trying to get it over with." The reason great lovers don't exist is because men have always had to get out of the bathroom quickly. If a man goes into a bathroom and he is there too long, people ask, "What are you doing in there?" or the guy thinks, "Oh no! They know what I am doing!"

If a woman is in the bathroom for a long time, people say, "Oh, she's putting on makeup, she's changing her clothes twenty-five times." A woman can spend as much time in the bathroom as she wishes. A man only gets about thirty seconds, and beating off in thirty seconds is not easy.

This is where you have to do the practice, "Okay, what is my sexual reality?" Have you ever questioned what your sexual reality is? With all the stuff you have in place about sex, you literally fry your brain if you ask, "What is my sexual reality?"

TS:

I have always chosen guys where I do it for them. I see how this plays out in my whole reality. I've never chosen my reality.

Gary:

If somebody needs something from you, you keep trying to provide what they need. We discovered with Dain that he has tried to give energy to every woman he has ever had sex with. That's quite a few women. That's a lot of energy he has to give. And he has to keep it there as long as he has even a vague inclination that they still exist. So, can he have *his* reality? Can he have his choice without considering them first? No. Now he can see the choice he is making, and that's major. If you can see the choice you are making, another possibility opens up. A different door becomes available to you.

The phenomenance of having your own sexual reality means you can choose more.

"I GIVE SO I DON'T HAVE TO RECEIVE"

Gary:

MT, your sexual reality is "I give so I don't have to receive."

MT:

Could you elaborate on that?

Gary:

How often do you try to give so you don't have to receive anything from anybody or take anything from anybody?

MT:

All the time.

Gary:

You have somewhere misidentified that receiving is eating shit.

MT:

Can we change that, please?

Gary:

You can change it by choosing, "I will not judge. I will make my life about receiving. My reality will be 'I will receive everything without judgment.'"

That's my reality. Someone can call me an asshole and I will say, "Yeah, because I am. Is there anything I am not? No. I can be everything." But you don't want to have the "labels" you have defined as "bad" as part of your reality. I want to have everything as part of my reality, because if I have everything as part of my reality, then I have total choice.

> *I want to have everything as part of my
> reality, because if I have everything as part
> of my reality, then I have total choice.*

DEFINING WHAT SEX IS

LY:

GN and I have been asking a lot of questions around sex since we have been here, and this morning, we realized how we had defined what sex is.

Gary:

What you had to do, what you could do, or what you couldn't do.

LY:

Yes. There were all kinds of definitions about what sex was for us. I didn't want him to go down on me, and he felt that he couldn't ejaculate unless he did it inside of me, and so on.

Gary:

This is exactly what I am talking about. We have all these definitions about how sex is supposed to be, and in those definitions there are no questions that give you a different possibility. There has to be a different possibility. My sense is that there is a different possibility available that could give you a space of choosing to go beyond any limitation into every possibility. And every possibility might look different than you think it does.

We have all these definitions about how sex is supposed to be and in those definitions, there are no questions that give you a different possibility.

EL:

Sex is one of my favorite subjects. I have played with pretty much everything along the sexual spectrum. For a few months I wasn't having sex with anyone. I was asking my body, and there just wasn't anyone it wanted to have sex with. Recently I created a lover and it was just awesome. The first night we got together, it was just frigging brilliant. It was so easy and fun.

I had to work the next day, so I kicked him out. I said, "You did really well, so you can come back tomorrow night if you like." Which he did, and it was awesome again. So two times. I was working again the next day, so I kicked him out and invited him back for the weekend. I tapped into Dain's energy and said, "I don't want to get into relationship with this." It was coming up on three times.

Gary:

Three times. The first time is for fun, the second time is for relationship, and the third time you are getting married, whether you think it is so or not. This goes on the menu for the male and the female plate. Three times, you're getting married. Bring in the U-Haul so we can move you.

EL:

He was an amazing gift to my body and so much fun, and he said he had never experienced the kind of space that he had with me and my body. We had a couple of conversations and I could feel myself tripping into relationship. What it is right now is that I can have whatever I want. He said, "Just call. My penis and I are here for you anytime." I don't have to be constrained. I have actually created exactly what I would like.

Gary:

And you are still not comfortable with it.

EL:

Yeah, what is that?

Gary:

Because you have to get what your sexual reality is.

What have you made so vital about never possessing the phenomenance of your sexual reality that keeps you stuck in human limitation? Everything that is times a godzillion, will you destroy and uncreate it all? Right and Wrong, Good and Bad, POD and POC, All 9, Shorts, Boys, and Beyonds.

Start asking what your sexual reality might be and do the Advanced Body Class so you can get the Phenomenance of Your Sexual Reality body process done—and see what starts to show up for you.

INDULGE THE FANTASIES

JH:

I love being in the relationship that I am in, but I sometimes want to have sex with other people. It would be great if once a week I could kiss someone different. But I don't think I could do that with the person I am with now. I find that uncomfortable.

Gary:

You got what your sexual reality is. You would like to kiss and have sex with somebody else. That is your sexual reality. Is that going to work for him? No. Does that mean you have to cut off that part of you? Or does that mean you just have to acknowledge that it is really a fun idea and it is not going to work with the person you're with, so you won't do it? You just say, "That is what I would like."

JH:

That makes me feel heaps better. I find the lying thing a bit funny. When I go home, he will look into my eyes and he will know and he will say, "Ugh."

Gary:

So your sexual reality is not "I get to lie." What if your sexual reality was "Well, I just won't tell him"?

JH:

A part of me wishes that, but I don't think I could do it.

Gary:

Well, maybe you only think you can't do it. Maybe you actually could, but never mind.

JH:

I wonder how people do that.

Gary:

The people who do that are kind of scary, because most of them do it out of meanness. They cheat in order to make the other person wrong.

JH:

Thank you. So just look and admire but don't touch.

Gary:

Yep. Enjoy, indulge the fantasy, and masturbate if you need to.

BF:

Having fantasies about other people has made sex with my partner a whole lot more fun.

JH:

Does he know that you do that?

BF:

Yeah, he does it, too.

JH:

While you are having sex?

BF:

Yeah.

JH:

I don't think my partner would understand that.

BF:

It is so much fun to go out and see someone who is really exciting.

JH:

So what do you do?

BF:

We'll go out and I can feel it in his body when he sees somebody that is a turn-on for him, and he will be really horny when we get home. I know that person's energy has revved him up, but who cares? And I do the same thing with and for him.

JH:

Fantastic.

Gary:

That's the pragmatics of relationship.

WAITING FOR PERMISSION

LD:

As we are talking about this, I realize that I grew up always waiting for permission for the right time. It was "Sex is great, but wait."

Gary:

Wait until the right person comes along?

LD:

Wait until you are married.

Gary:

Oh that.

LD:

I didn't buy into that, fortunately, but I realize that I transferred it into "Things have to be right. A man has to be right."

Gary:

So you actually did buy it.

LD:

I did, but I transferred it into something else. And that sucks because waiting for permission to have sex is...

Gary:

Hopefully the Phenomenance of Your Sexual Reality process will begin to unlock that for you. I hope to get all of you to the point where you are at ground zero, and "What would I like to create as my life?" is your mantra. Every day you wake up in the morning and ask, "What would I like to create as my life today?" It's not based on anybody else's point of view, and it's not based on anything that you *have* to do. It's based on the choices that are available to you and the possibilities of everything that can be that you have not yet chosen.

What have you made so vital about never possessing the phenomenance of your sexual reality that keeps you stuck in human insanity? Everything that is times a godzillion, will you destroy and uncreate it all? Right and Wrong, Good and Bad, POD and POC, All 9, Shorts, Boys, and Beyonds.

What have you made so vital about never possessing the phenomenance of your sexual reality that keeps you stuck in the insanity of human reality? Everything that is times a godzillion, will you destroy and uncreate it all? Right and Wrong, Good and Bad, POD and POC, All 9, Shorts, Boys, and Beyonds.

"What would I like to create as my life today?"

NOBODY IS GOING TO NOTICE

Some of you are going to say, "But if I have my reality, I am going to get punished or destroyed." No, if you have your reality, nobody is going to notice. Why? Because people have created everything about you based on their judgments of how you are like them. And when they meet you, they will judge that you fit into that.

It will be very easy for you to know what you need to say to them so they can feel comfortable with you. All of you have this ability already but you are not using it because you get accused of being a chameleon. Being a chameleon is a great thing; it's not a wrongness. It means you know how to make other people feel comfortable enough to take advantage of them. Why wouldn't you take advantage of everything that you had available to you? Yet you won't have your sexual reality because that would mean you would be taking advantage of people. You see that as a wrongness.

It's like if you ladies went out and grabbed some guy and used him wantonly, by human reality that would mean you are a terrible person, right? So you won't do it when you want to because it is wrong for you to want to do it. But a man wants to be used that way.

What have you made so vital about never possessing the phenomenance of your sexual reality that keeps you stuck in the insanity of human reality? Everything that is times a godzillion, will you destroy and uncreate it all? Right and Wrong, Good and Bad, POD and POC, All 9, Shorts, Boys, and Beyonds.

Little kids come in with a sexual reality—and then it gets killed.

How many of you had a sexual reality when you were a kid and it got killed dynamically? Everything that does not allow you to reinstitute that and have your own reality, will you destroy and uncreate it all? Right and Wrong, Good and Bad, POD and POC, All 9, Shorts, Boys, and Beyonds.

KC:

If a woman wantonly has sex with a man, it means she is wrong. Isn't there also a big judgment of the man if he enjoys it?

Gary:

He'll love it—until he talks to his friends. His friends will make him wrong for it.

KC:

And then he has to be angry with the woman because he received that judgment. And I, as the woman, would take that as the wrongness of enjoying sex, because he is coming back with all this judgment.

Gary:

And where's your sexual reality in that? Your sexual reality becomes "What judgment do I have to deal with in order to have sex?" How is that good? It's not.

Everything that is times a godzillion, will you destroy and uncreate it all? Right and Wrong, Good and Bad, POD and POC, All 9, Shorts, Boys, and Beyonds.

This is all part of human reality's point of view. If you don't have your own sexual reality, you will go into this. It was very fortunate for me that when I was a kid, I decided I was going to be a virgin when I got married … until I hit twenty-one and realized, "I don't want to be a virgin." So I went after a girl who was a known slut in the place where I worked. She wouldn't date anybody at work, but I got her to go out with me. I learned about sex from that girl! We had sex in every space and every place and in every position known to mankind. That was my first sexual experience. I thought she was wonderful and I would have stayed with her forever except that my friends said, "You can't marry a slut like that."

I said, "Oh." My friends didn't approve of her.

Later I created a sexual reality, where if my male friends didn't approve, I would keep the woman. I knew that if my male friends didn't approve, she was the right girl for me. My sexual reality is always to choose someone who is a total slut because sluts are more fun. I had way more fun in sex than anybody I knew. That was my reality. So I personally appreciate every person who is willing to be a slut because I know ultimately they are willing to have fun.

"JUST FOR ME, JUST FOR FUN, AND NEVER TELL ANYONE"

LB:

What comes up for me is that my sexual reality is selective.

Gary:

That's not your sexual reality.

LB:

So I have made it mine?

Gary:

Yes. A sexual reality would not be selective or exclusionary. It would be inclusionary of all possibilities and it would be a question.

LB:

I don't have that. I judge a lot.

Gary:

And are the judgments yours? Or are they what you have been taught?

LB:

They are what I have been taught.

Gary:

You are supposed to get married and have children. Did you manage that? Yes. And you married within your culture.

LB:

I think for me it was for convenience. It was more convenient for me to marry him.

Gary:

What is your sexual reality that you don't want to know? This question is for all of you. What is your true sexual reality that you don't want to know? That you never want to know and that if you knew it would blow your mind and everybody else's?

Everything that is times a godzillion, will you destroy and uncreate it all? Right and Wrong, Good and Bad, POD and POC, All 9, Shorts, Boys, and Beyonds.

And by the way, when you find your sexual reality, please don't tell people. It's "Just for me, just for fun, and never tell anyone."

What have you made so vital about repressing, suppressing, and eradicating your sexual reality that if you actually chose it, you think you would die? That's why you won't choose it. Everything that is times a godzillion, will you destroy and uncreate it all? Right and Wrong, Good and Bad, POD and POC, All 9, Shorts, Boys, and Beyonds.

DW:

What do you mean by that?

Gary:

By refusing to have your reality, you validate other people's realities as true and real, and yours as not real. In so doing, you stick them with their reality even if it isn't working. That's not a kindness. The greatest kindness you can have is having your own reality.

What have you made so vital about repressing, suppressing, and eradicating your sexual reality that if you chose it, you think you would die? Everything that is times a godzillion, will you destroy and uncreate it all? Right and Wrong, Good and Bad, POD and POC, All 9, Shorts, Boys, and Beyonds.

LB:

What comes up for me is that I don't mind dying.

Gary:

You would rather die than have your own sexual reality.

LB:

Yes, it is the way I work. It might be torture or something.

Gary:

No, that's your justification. If you don't tell anybody, you can't be tortured for it. You guys have this weird point of view that if you do something you think is inappropriate, everybody is going to know. That's because you keep putting a sign over your head that flashes in big neon lights:

"Secret Here. Secret Here. Secret Here." Everybody is asking, "What is it that you are hiding?"

When you find your sexual reality, please don't tell people. It's "Just for me, just for fun, and never tell anyone."

THINK WILDLY, DRESS CONVENTIONALLY

I had a friend who used to say, "Think wildly, dress conventionally." If you dress conventionally, people will have no idea how wild your mind is. If you dress extravagantly, you are exposing the fact that you aren't normal. Look conventional, think wildly, and nobody will ever question you. And if you are being you, nobody is ever going to notice they can't stop you.

LB:

That doesn't mean hide?

Gary:

People are not interested in you. When you have the point of view that you need to hide something, you think that what you are doing is so interesting that everybody will notice. But nobody is interested. You say, "I don't want to be judged!" Nobody is going to notice. You keep thinking that everybody is going to pay attention to what you are doing. Nobody pays attention to what you are doing. They're paying attention to what *they* are doing and thinking that everybody is going to judge *them* for.

LB:

I feel like I am putting it out there psychically in some way.

Gary:

You are creating a place and a space in you where everything begins to reflect the judgment, not the possibility.

LB:

That is true.

Gary:

All you have to do is ask a question: "What possibilities are being created with this judgment?" None! Then you begin to see that judgment has no value. You're making judgment more valuable than you. That is not one of your brightest, smartest moments. In the different wattages of bulbs, you are a seven-and-a-half watt bulb. That's a little tiny spark of light. If you're a 250-watt light, you blind everybody and they can't look at you.

LB:

That is an awesome perspective and possibility. I love that.

PR:

What if you could have sex from total consciousness? What is that?

Gary:

It is never having a point of view even during the act of sex and never trying to get a point of view to figure out what you are going to do. It's being willing to be in the question of "What can this person's body receive and what can my body receive that I have never chosen?" From that, you might create your own sexual reality. Might! If you don't have your sexual reality, all you have is the reality of judgment.

What can this person's body receive and what can my body receive that I have never chosen?

SEXUAL HEALING

NJ:

Now that we're talking about sexual reality, can you talk about sexual healing?

Gary:

If you are a sexual healer, you tend to choose people who are screwed up and you try to heal them sexually. That might not be your best choice. A better choice might be doing something that is nurturing to your body and your soul.

Sexual healing is one of the capacities most of us have, and we tend to pick messed up people to have sex with. If you are someone who continues to pick screwed-up and judgmental people to have sex with, you are probably doing sexual healing, and you might want to ask, "Okay body, can we stop doing that and now have a little nurturance and fun and caring and joyful stuff? A little fun and joyful copulation?"

MA:

How can I talk to my students about sexual healing?

Gary:

Just mention it straight on. It's amazing. The kids will get it and they will say, "Really? No wonder I always like people who are mean to me." Make it simple for them. How old are they?

MA:

I usually talk to kids between fourteen and eighteen.

Gary:

Perfect. They need that information, because it's hard to be a teenager. They are not quite old enough to screw their brains loose and they want to. And they're too young to be able to get away with just petting. In this day and age, you are supposed to start having sex at twelve.

What have you made so vital about never possessing the phenomenance of copulatory reality that keeps you choosing fucked up people to have fucking with? Everything that is times a godzillion, will you destroy and uncreate it all? Right and Wrong, Good and Bad, POD and POC, All 9, Shorts, Boys, and Beyonds.

You think it's much more fun to have "Who can I copulate with today?" than "Who could nurture my body?" There are lots more people who will copulate with you than will nurture your body. Have you ever noticed? But you are not willing to have the phenomenance of what copulation could truly be. The phenomenance of magnificent copulation.

Do you get that you haven't asked for that ... ever? You have asked, "Who can I fuck? Who can fuck me? Who can I have sex with? Who? Who? Who?" You are not an owl. Everything that is times a godzillion, will you destroy and uncreate it all? Right and Wrong, Good and Bad, POD and POC, All 9, Shorts, Boys, and Beyonds.

PR:

What's coming up for me is all the times I tried to sexually heal somebody who didn't want to receive it. A lot of it is stuff with previous lives.

Gary:

You've been trying to create a reality that matches somebody else's instead of finding your own. Most people find a person who matches their reality and then they try to create a relationship with that person. Instead of asking, "What's this going to create?" and "Where is this going to lead?" they go to the conclusion "This person will be the perfect partner." The thing is there is no such thing as a perfect partner except for this ten seconds. And it better last longer than ten seconds or you'll want to dump them. That's a Hollywood marriage.

What have you made so vital about possessing the phenomenance of the lies, lines, limitations, and judgments and the thoughts, feelings, and emotions of human reality as your reality that keeps you stuck in the gristmill of human reality? Everything that is times a godzillion, will you destroy and uncreate it all? Right and Wrong, Good and Bad, POD and POC, All 9, Shorts, Boys, and Beyonds.

> *You think it's much more fun to have*
> *"Who can I copulate with today?"*
> *than "Who could nurture my body?"*

YOU HAVE TO HAVE YOUR SEXUAL REALITY IF YOU ARE GOING TO CREATE YOUR REALITY

TS:

This conversation is one of the most intense things ever. It is exploding everything I have made real in my life.

Gary:

You have tried to make it real, but it has never really been real, has it?

TS:

No.

Gary:

You knew it didn't quite work, but you had no idea why.

TS:

Exactly.

Gary:

You thought it was supposed to create everything that everybody told you it would create, but it didn't.

TS:

(in tears) It is like being a hamster in a hamster wheel.

Gary:

How is that creating your reality? Is that kind of sadness and tears your reality?

TS:

No.

Gary:

No, you have a better sense of humor than that. What if you started looking at what was funny about it instead of what is wrong with it?

TS:

That is usually my way of being.

Gary:

Oh, you mean that is part of your reality?

TS:

So what is the part of just wanting to kill everything and everyone?

Gary:

It is called justifiable insanity.

TS:

What do you mean?

Gary:

How many people in the world are worthwhile or fun to hang out with? Not enough.

TS:

(laughing) I don't know why this is so funny.

Gary:

Isn't it phenomenal the way people judge? Yeah. They are really good at it.

What have you made so vital about possessing the phenomenance of lies, judgments, limitations, thoughts, feelings, and emotions that keeps you stuck in the gristmill of human reality? Everything that is times a godzillion, will you destroy and uncreate it all? Right and Wrong, Good and Bad, POD and POC, All 9, Shorts, Boys, and Beyonds.

TS:

Since I was a little kid, I have gone around looking at people and asking, "How is he or she seeing this, and if I see it my way, what is it going to create as a reaction in that person?" I go from wanting to say, "Can we play? Can we have fun?" to bastardising it into referencing how they are reacting to whatever it is, as in "Oh, what do you think about this?"

Gary:

Would you look at something here? You were smart enough to do that. Many people are not. You were able to recognize that they were doing something and that they were reacting.

TS:

I thought everyone did that.

Gary:

"I thought that everyone had that capacity."

TS:

I have never seen it as a capacity.

Gary:

If you don't see it as a capacity, you can't choose it as part of your reality. "Oh good, I can see when people are idiots." There is a sixth sense where you can see dead people like the kid in the movie, *The Sixth Sense,* and then there's the seventh sense, where you can see stupid people.

TS:

So what would it take for me to turn this into an entertainment?

Gary:

It is not about entertainment. It's about "How do I use this to my advantage?" This made your life easier when you were a kid, but did you make it right or wrong?

TS:

Wrong.

Gary:

When you start acknowledging that you can do that and you have that awareness, you can figure out how you can use it. As long as you keep trying to figure out how you can use it, you will be in a state of creation.

TS:

And if I don't see this as a capacity, I make myself the victim of it? That is where I felt stuck and locked up. So the question is, "Can I use this to my advantage?"

Gary:

What did all of you have as capacities that you labeled "wrongness" that keep you from having them and being them today? Everything that is times a godzillion, will you destroy and uncreate it all? Right and Wrong, Good and Bad, POD and POC, All 9, Shorts, Boys, and Beyonds.

TS:

This is something I haven't even received as a gift and as a capacity. It is so easy to see this as about other people. I meet people and say, "Yeah, there it is."

Gary:

But you assume you must be like them or they must be like you.

TS:

Yes, exactly.

Gary:

What if they are neither like you, nor not like you?

TS:

That is exactly the point.

Gary:

How much judgment is there in "They must be like me or I must be like them?"

TS:

Tons.

Gary:

Or is it all judgment? What if you were willing to recognize "I have this capacity. Now what do I do with it?"

TS:

Thank you! This is so big in my universe—how I constantly try to reference and like things.

Gary:

Yep. You like to like. Do you like liking people?

TS:

No.

Gary:

The reality is that you don't like people. You can understand them and you can see what they are functioning from. That's the awareness that can be your reality if you are willing to choose it. And sex is the one place where you will always shut it off.

TS:

Yes.

Gary:

Which is why you have to have your sexual reality if you are going to create your reality, period.

SM:

Thank you so much.

What if your sexual reality was not just men or just women but the sexual energy of every moment of every day? Orgasmic living is more true to what true sexualness is than anything else.

The Creative Edge of Possibility

COMMUNION IS WITH ALL THINGS

ND:

Will you talk about communion with regard to phenomenance?

Gary:

People say, "I want to have communion with this person," and for them, having communion with a particular person means "I want a relationship." That's not communion. Communion is with all things, not an individual. As you begin to create your reality you will have a sense, an awareness, of what actually can become possible. That's total communion. It's the awareness of all that is possible. When you do communion, when you are being communion, you are unable to choose anything but phenomenance.

RR:

You have talked about how we are trying to create followers rather than people to play with. I can see that, and I want you to talk more about creating people to play with. If we are not playing with each other, how can we think that we're ever going to achieve communion?

Gary:

Yes, communion begins when you play with everybody who shows up in your life. Who do I exclude?

RR:

Nobody.

Gary:

How do I play with you? Sometimes I flirt. Sometimes I make comments. Sometimes I give you a wedgie. It is always done in play. I'm not trying to control. I ask, "Where is this choice going to lead?" If I choose to flirt with you, is that going to lead someplace?

RR:

Why do you flirt with me?

Gary:

Because it's fun. Sometimes it confuses you and I love the look of confusion on your face. It's as if you're asking, "Does this mean something I don't get?"

RR:

But there's nothing to get, right? It's just fun?

Gary:

It's just fun. If you did everything from the fun of it and it had no meaning, how much easier would your life be?

Communion is with all things, not an individual.

CONNECTION AND COMMUNION

DW:

Can you talk about connection and communion?

Gary:

If you have *communion,* you have connection with everything. If you don't have communion, you have connection with nothing. Everything that you call *connection* is a contrivance to pretend you have created something.

DW:

If I am in communion with everything and I go for a walk in the bush, it's great. Then I come back and I'm around people, and I want to be out in the forest again.

Gary:

What if you had the same kind of connection and communion with people that you had with the forest? If you are out in the bush and there is a poisonous bush, do you touch it?

DW:

No.

Gary:

How do you know it is poisonous?

DW:

You just know.

Gary:

But if you meet people, you assume they can't be as bad as you think they are. They can't be as bad as you know they are. Because all people are basically good, right?

Everything you have done to make yourself feel connected, and everything you have done to eliminate communion, will you destroy and uncreate all that? Right and Wrong, Good and Bad, POD and POC, All 9, Shorts, Boys, and Beyonds.

DW:

I once had an amazing session with Dain, and afterward when I walked outside, it was like everyone was sleeping.

Gary:

Most people are sleeping. The majority of people sleepwalk. They are not present. They are not in connection with anything. They are not in communion with anything and they function as though they are the most brilliant creatures upon the planet. Brains are a dangerous thing. People believe that because they can think, they are smarter than everything and everyone else. Just be aware that people are asleep. "Oh, that person's asleep. I'd better not walk in front of him or I might get squashed."

I am always aware that ninety percent of the people walk down the street without seeing anything. They have made themselves deaf, dumb, and blind. Why would you choose that? You have the awareness that they are not present in life. And when you are aware, you have an advantage over them.

As you begin to create your reality you will have a sense, an
awareness, of what actually can become possible.
That's total communion. It's the
awareness of all that is possible.

USING THIS REALITY TO YOUR ADVANTAGE

ND:

This morning I was looking at functioning outside of this reality. There is something—almost a divide—between this reality and what's beyond this reality. How do I create a sense of harmony with this reality?

Gary:

You don't want harmony with this reality. Harmony with this reality would be aligning and agreeing with it in some way. Nor do you want to resist and react to this reality, which would be "I've got to get rid of it." You just want to know how to use it: "How can I use this reality to my advantage?"

ND:

I keep trying to create a sense of harmony with this reality.

Gary:

Believing in harmony is as crazy as believing in fairness.

ND:

What does it look like when you are functioning outside of this reality and...

Gary:

Ask: "How can I practice my own reality?" Practice, practice, practice. Practice makes perfect. The idea is that if you continue to practice, what might be possible? Something greater can occur. What would that be like? Practice, practice. What can I practice to live in my own reality? What practice can I do or be today that would create my own reality right away?

It has nothing to do with harmony. It has to do with the communion of all things. You've got two horses out here. Are you going to plough fields or ride away?

ND:

Ride away.

Gary:

It's just a choice. Are you functioning as an infinite being—or are you trying to function from this reality?

ND:

That.

Gary:

That's the one that will kill you, folks. Don't function from this reality. Function from beyond this reality and use this reality to your advantage.

What have you made so vital about never possessing the phenomenance of advantage that keeps you disempowering you? Everything that is times a godzillion, will you destroy and uncreate it all? Right and Wrong, Good and Bad, POD and POC, All 9, Shorts, Boys, and Beyonds.

What have you made so vital about never possessing the phenomenance of advantage that keeps you disempowering and abdicating infinite possibility as you? Everything that is times a godzillion, will you destroy and uncreate it all? Right, Wrong, Good and Bad, POD and POC, All 9, Shorts, Boys, and Beyonds.

Don't function from this reality.
Function from beyond this reality and
use this reality to your advantage.

BE A PREDATOR

AK:

Many years ago, you gave me a clearing about being a predator: "What energy space and consciousness can my body and I be, to be the velociraptor I truly be?" The willingness to be the predator has changed a lot for me. Not only to be the predator but to do it with joy. Nature's got a lot of predators.

Gary:

Yes, the funny part is that most of you are trying to pretend you are not predators while actually being predators. You are frigging humanoids. You are predators of magnitude. What's the one animal that never gets attacked by others? Humanoids. Why? Because they will always attack first. Are you living like that or enjoying that?

What have you made so vital about never possessing the phenomenance of advantage that keeps you disempowering, disabling, and abdicating everything that is valuable about you to somebody else's reality? Everything that is times a godzillion, will you destroy and uncreate it all? Right and Wrong, Good and Bad, POD and POC, All 9, Shorts, Boys, and Beyonds.

MA was talking with me about how everybody wants to fight him, and I said, "You have got to learn to be intimidating." He asked me what I meant by that and I said, "You have to walk like you own the world. Learn to walk the way your mom walks. She walks into a room and everybody says, 'Oh!' You walk into the room and everybody says, 'How can I beat the shit out of this guy?' She's doing intimidation. You're doing 'I can be intimidated.' Be willing to walk into the room, owning it. People will want to attack you if you can be intimidated."

I asked him to walk a little different. I showed him a different possibility and he walked in here and he got instant validation of it. People looked at him and acted differently around him. You've all got to do that.

THE PHENOMENANCE OF ADVANTAGE

DT:

Can you talk more about the phenomenance of advantage?

Gary:

When you don't take advantage of a situation, you are actually disempowering you. For example, do you have an ability to see the possibilities in stocks and investments? Do you use that to your advantage? Are you willing to see what other people will choose?

DT:

Yes.

Gary:

And does seeing what other people will choose give you a different point of view about how you invest?

DT:

Yes.

Gary:

And in so doing have you made less money or more money?

DT:

More money.

Gary:

Yes, because you are willing to dump something if it is not working. You are willing to create something if it is working. You are willing to look at any possibility rather than thinking it is a particular way.

DT:

Yes.

Gary:

So when do you allow yourself to be even greater? When you are predatory or when you are not?

DT:

Predatory.

Gary:

The willingness to be predatory is the willingness to go in and do whatever it takes to get whatever you want. It's never sitting around waiting for somebody else to take advantage or eat you in any direction. It's always knowing that you have an awareness of something that other people don't have. I am a predator of magnitude. I never assume I am going to be eaten unless I choose it. I always assume that I am going to be the consumer not the consumed. And guess what? That's what happens.

When do you allow yourself to be even greater? When you are predatory, when you're willing to go for the advantage— or when you disempower yourself?

DT:

When I'm predatory.

Gary:

What have you made so vital about never possessing the phenomenance of advantage that keeps you disempowering, abdicating, and disabling everything that is valuable about you to somebody else's reality? Everything that is times a godzillion, will you destroy and uncreate it all? Right, Wrong, Good and Bad, POD and POC, All 9, Shorts, Boys, and Beyonds.

When you don't take advantage of a situation,
you are actually disempowering you.

WHERE DO YOU WANT TO CREATE YOUR LIFE FROM ?

NK:

Do you have to know what you are going for?

Gary:

You have to get where you want to create your life and your reality from. Have you created your life from kind of, a little bit of, a lot of, or an exceptional amount of victim?

NK:

All of those.

Gary:

Is that working for you?

NK:

It's absolutely not working.

Gary:

If you became predatory, you wouldn't be victimized by your family's saying, "Maybe we will give you money, maybe we will leave you money, maybe you will get something in the future." If you were predatory, would you have a need of them? No. Would their need to get you to agree with them increase or decrease? It would increase. Being the predator, you'd have control. They couldn't get what they wanted unless they gave you what you wanted.

What have you made so vital about never possessing the phenomenance of advantage that keeps you disempowering you? Everything that is times a godzillion, will you destroy and uncreate it all? Right and Wrong, Good and Bad, POD and POC, All 9, Shorts, Boys, and Beyonds.

THE BLESSED POSSIBILITY OF COMPETITION

ND:

I realized recently that I love to work hard. I like to push my limits.

Gary:

Why?

ND:

I feel like a racehorse running. I like to feel my infiniteness. To be my infiniteness.

Gary:

You like to head up the pack. You want to outrun everybody ... not that you are competitive.

ND:

Is this just all a fun choice—or is there something weird here?

Gary:

It's a fun choice. You've got to realize, "I like to compete. I like to go as fast as I can. I like to get ahead of the troops with great ease. Okay cool, that's what I like." Then you have to ask: "What could I create or choose that would be even greater than this?"

ND:

I think I do competition mostly with myself. Is that just plain dumb? Or is that a contribution in some way?

Gary:

Well, that is not looking at all of the aspects. What would be the blessed possibility of competition? What are the possibilities with competition that you have never acknowledged or used?

ND:

But "No Competition" is one of the ten commandments of Access.

Gary:

The commandment, "No Competition" is about the way competition is done in this reality. It means don't bad-mouth others, because most competition in this reality is about bad-mouthing other people. People vilify somebody else to prove they are better. That does not create; that destroys. The primary thing it destroys is your own business. When you have to bad-mouth somebody else to prove you are better, all you are proving is that you are less—and people know it. When you lie, people know it. Don't lie, and don't withhold information unless they can't hear it, which isn't lying.

What would be the blessed possibility of competition?
What are the possibilities with competition that
you have never acknowledged or used?

THE CREATIVE EDGE

Competition in this reality is about taking what somebody else has produced and doing it better. True competition is "How can I out-create what this person is creating? How can I create more consciousness than anybody else can create?" That's the blessed possibility of competition.

ND:

Thank you. I was thinking that to be the phenomenance, there had to be some competition. Is that a lie?

Gary:

Competition can be a choice. You are making it into an either/or universe; you either do it or you don't do it. And you judge whether you are doing it or you are not doing it.

That is judgment, not competition, and judgment always destroys what you are trying to create.

That's the reason you have had areas in your life where you feel like you are doing jerks and starts. You start to go gangbusters and then it fails, because instead of asking, "How can I out-create myself?" you go to "This person is competing with me." "This person is competing with me" is what question? It's not a question. You are coming to conclusion, and when you come to conclusion, the only thing that is possible is less.

ND:

So what would be the question to ask?

Gary:

How can I use my competitive edge to create everything I want and to get my minions to work harder for me? It's good to have minions.

The *cutting* edge is where you cut out other people from success. Cutting edge means you have to be ahead of the game. The *creative* edge is where you create for you *and* for everybody else. Creative edge means you are the game. A completely different universe can exist when you're functioning from the creative edge of possibility. If you are not willing to be the creative edge, you can't have phenomenance.

A completely different universe can exist when you're functioning from the creative edge of possibility. If you are not willing to be the creative edge, you can't have phenomenance.

349

The Phenomenance of Magic, Change, and Choice

Gary:

Dain had a difficult day yesterday. He had a huge sense of expansion and possibility but he couldn't figure out how to take people there, because not enough people were willing to go. And we will usually make the ones who aren't willing to go more vital and important that the ones who are. Think about it in terms of a mountain. You want to get to the top with everyone. But is everybody going to want to get to the top? No, not everybody will, but if you start leading towards the top, those who can't go more than 100 feet will stop at 100 feet. Those who can only do 200 feet will stop at 200 feet. Those who can only do 300 feet will stop at 300 feet. You never stop you in favor of those who cannot go.

Dain:

That's what I was doing. I looked into everybody's worlds and I said, "I don't think I can do this. I don't think I can take everyone to the space I have learned is possible." And with that one conclusion, I started shutting myself down.

Gary:

One conclusion shuts you down. Don't do that.

Dain:

I second that! Don't do that. With that one conclusion, I made me as small as I could be so I fit everybody's space. If I had come from the new space I knew was possible, if I had come from the new universe I knew was possible to create, what would I have been and done? I wouldn't have tried to force people to go there. I wouldn't have tried to put up barriers. I would have said, "Hi. I have found this new thing. Come on, let's go. Let's play. It's okay if you don't want to." Since then, my question has been: "If I were to be this new reality I now have available, in this situation, what would be different?" And it's changing everything.

Gary:

You are an acoustical wavelength of change and possibility that you have not yet acknowledged or seen. You don't see the waves of acoustical possibility that you create by being you at the moment you are being you, because other people can't acknowledge that. They can't see it, they can't recognize it—but they can change.

CF:

Dain and I were in the lift with a Japanese woman. Dain said, "Hello, how beautiful you are," and he instantly changed her reality. MN said, "Acknowledge how you can change the reality of people in an instant, just like that."

Gary:

This world is not set up to acknowledge or receive. If you will acknowledge and receive every person that comes into your reality, you will change everything. This is a talent. This is an ability. This is a phenomenance called *you*.

JUST BE THE PHENOMENANCE

PR:

How do you suggest we speak about phenomenance with the rest of the world?

Gary:

You don't have to talk about it. *Just be it*. You can run processes if you have friends you think can receive them. Be willing to run the processes on people who can receive them. Don't run the processes on those who can't.

LM:

When I become aware of something that nobody else has been aware of, I tend to want to share it with others.

Gary:

But you don't ask a question. You just want to take people along. If all people want is the first 100 feet of the mountain, you keep trying to take them all the way to the top. No. You need to ask, "What part of this can they receive?"

LM:

Right, and if you create in your own way, then those who take it on, take it on, and those who don't, don't—and that's fine.

Gary:

Yes, because they will get there when they choose and you will get there when you choose. It is *when* not *if*, because you will not give up. You tend to wish more for others than they wish for themselves. This is the most important thing to get. If you have children, you know that place. If you don't have children, then you have friends that you wish more for than you do for yourself. You wish more for your family and your friends, but are they willing to have the more that you are willing to wish for? No.

"CAN THESE PEOPLE GO WHERE I WANT TO TAKE THEM?"

Dain:

So how is it possible for me and for us to have more ease with that?

Gary:

The first thing you have to do is recognize it. That's the purpose of the question, "Can these people go where I want to take them?" No. "Where can they go?" "Oh, okay, they can go 100 feet. This one can go 200 feet. This bunch can go 300 feet. Oh, and this one person can go all the way to the top." Stop assuming you can take everyone to the top. You are not a beast of burden. How many of you have signed yourself up as the beast of burden who must take everyone with you? You're not the jackass of consciousness.

Back in the seventies, I went to Morocco and there were light, little donkeys that had huge stacks of wood on them. The stacks of wood were so huge you couldn't see the donkeys' heads. As you went behind them, you could see their tails. As you went past them, you could see four little legs walking along. There was a guy sitting on top of the stack of wood beating the donkey to get it to go forward. I would look at this and say, "Really?" That is the way you guys look to me.

Dain:

That's the way we feel sometimes, too.

Gary:

The question is "Who is sitting on top of you beating you forward?"

Dain:

Oh, that's not you?

Gary:

No!

Dain:

Well, if it's not you up there, I am over it. I don't need to do it anymore.

Gary:

Good!

Dain:

I know that it ultimately boils down to choice and the awareness of it.

Stop assuming you can take everyone to the top.
You are not a beast of burden.

YOU HAVE TO CHOOSE IT

Gary:

Everybody wants me to POD and POC it, but I can't. You have to choose it. That's the reason I want to give you the vision of what is actually possible for you, the world, and universe that you are capable of creating that you haven't chosen yet.

Dain:

So it is not vital that we get everyone else to go?

Gary:

No. It is not necessary, it is not vital, it is not a need, it is not a requirement. You go with those who can play. You ask, "Who can play with me up in the stratosphere?" It's a different reality.

VT:

I am grateful for that because I have been so frustrated when I see people *can* do it, but the question is *"Will* they do it?"

Gary:

That's the question you've got to live with.

VT:

That's big. Thank you for bringing that up. There are so many people I work with in business. I see they *can* do it—but *will* they?

Gary:

Is it *potential* or *possibility*? You've got to identify it correctly. If you talk about it as potential, it is never going to come to fruition. But if you talk about it as *possibility*, it might. People can't change *potential*, but they can choose and change *possibility*.

VT:

All of that is possible and they still don't choose it. What's that about?

Gary:

They can't see it. You don't get that you are willing to see what other people will never see. All of you have always been able to see what other people can't see.

If you talk about it as potential, it is never going to come to fruition.
But if you talk about it as possibility, it might.

A PLACE OF ALLOWANCE WITH WHAT PEOPLE WILL NOT CHOOSE

Dain:

You know that thing about seeing what is actually possible for people and they're not choosing it? I realize there are things Gary saw that I could have chosen almost fifteen years ago, but even if he had drawn me a detailed map of it, I wouldn't have been able to read it.

Gary:

I did draw a detailed map! And you said, "I don't like this part."

Dain:

Yeah, I said, "Just take off that part about infinite possibilities." This conversation helps me personally because I see I wouldn't have been able to choose those things back then. When I started traveling with Gary, after the first night of a class he would be dejected and depressed because of where people couldn't go. He had the same thing—because people wouldn't go there—and over the years, I have seen him come to a place of allowance with what people will not choose.

Gary:

You have to choose allowance for what people cannot and will not choose.

Dain:

And the awareness of what may or may not be chosen in the future. If you are in allowance of it, it opens the door for it to possibly be chosen.

ND:

Isn't there a gift in them not choosing?

Gary:

The gift would be seeing what they are not going to choose. If they don't choose, you have to know that they can't choose or they won't choose. It's not "There is something wrong with me." Dain—and some of you—tend to think it is your fault if the other person doesn't choose it. You think you didn't do what you should have done or you didn't create what you should have created. You didn't say or do the thing that would have made them choose it. Wanting to make somebody choose doesn't work.

I wanted Dain to choose a lot of stuff for a long time, and he didn't choose it. I wanted all of my kids to choose it. I wanted each one of you to choose, and you didn't do it. But it's your choice, it's your life, and you have to choose. It can't be my choice. It's difficult to know that you would choose different for people and they won't choose it for themselves. That's the hard part for those of us who want to make the world sing. It's about the symphony of infinite possibilities. When you are willing to have the symphony of possibilities, you work in collaboration with consciousness to create greater possibilities.

It's difficult to know that you would choose different for people and they won't choose it for themselves. That's the hard part for those of us who want to make the whole world sing.

WHISPERS OF THE FUTURE

SL:

Gary, there have been a lot of times when you and Dain have done your best to show me the possibilities I didn't get. I am really grateful that you kept doing it.

Gary:

Yes, you would give up on you before I would give up on you.

SL:

I know and I am really grateful that you didn't give up on me because it's getting easier. Would you talk about the whispers of the future?

Gary:

The future is created in each choice you make. The whispers of the future that will be are the strongest element of possibility that exists at the moment of your choice. They will speak to you if you are willing to hear them. It's a choice you have to make. You don't try to control the future, nor do you try to make it go in the direction it's going to go. You simply ask the question: "What future is available here that I have not yet considered?"

SL:

Is that the listening you have talked about?

Gary:

That's the listening.

SL:

Cool. Thank you.

Gary:

The phenomenance of change is the magic that creates a different possibility. True magic is the constant states of possibility and choosing what is possible that nobody else can choose. Real magic is choosing what other people can't choose. That's the way I live my life. That's how I pragmatically deal with it. I have no idea what's going to show up in my life, but I'm grateful when it does.

"What future is available here that
I have not yet considered?"

THE PHENOMENANCE OF THE NINE TRANNIES AND ALL FORMS OF MAGIC

HB:

I know you have a willingness to be in connection with magic, I'll call it that, and I know it becomes greater for you all the time. And the world that you look into is totally life-giving.

Gary:

I have a process I want to run.

HB:

Let's do it.

Gary:

When you are willing to step up to phenomenance, you get to the place where you begin to see what your reality is. You begin to create your reality, regardless of anybody's point of view.

What have you made so vital about avoiding the magnificence and the phenomenance of the nine trannies and all forms of magic beyond that would give you the gift you are to the world? Everything that is times a godzillion, will you destroy and uncreate it all? Right and Wrong, Good and Bad, POD and POC, All 9, Shorts, Boys, and Beyonds.

The nine trannies are: transformation, transmigration, transfiguration, transexualness, transpiration, transmutation, translocation, transliteration, and transmogrification.

- *Transformation* is the ability to change anything from what it is now into something different.
- *Transmigration* is the ability to move from one location to another without a car, plane, train, or bus. It's migrating across space (not time). If you have ever had the experience of driving somewhere in a car and getting

there in a shorter period of time than you should have, you have been transmigrating—not folding time, but folding space.

+ *Transfiguration* is the ability to morph something from what it appears to be into something different.

+ *Transsexualness* is the ability to change the sexual energy of any moment or anything at will. It does not mean you are changing your genitalia. It means you don't function from your sexuality as the source of your reality. Sexuality always requires judgment.

+ *Transpiration* is the ability to change something that is going to transpire in the future and change it into something that doesn't have to be, so something else can occur.

+ *Transmutation* is the ability to change something from what it currently is into something you would like it to be. It's a mutation from what it is into something greater.

+ *Translocation* is moving something from one location to another.

+ *Transliteration* is talking in any language and understanding all languages.

+ *Transmogrification* is shifting what you look like into something different. It is shape shifting; for example, you could change yourself from being a man to a woman.

You do these things, and most of the time nobody notices because their point of view is that it can't be true. Most people seek validation for what they can do; they think that what makes them valuable is somebody noticing what they've done, but when you are willing to be the nine trannies, you no longer have to seek validation. When these things show up for you, do not ask how they happened. Instead ask:

+ What would it take for more of this to show up in my life?
+ What would I have to be in order for more of this to show up nonstop?

HB:

When you talk about the nine trannies, a huge resistance comes up in my universe, and I don't usually resist anything. It is weird to feel that resistance. I have had a resistance against the nine trannies ever since you started talking about them. I never want to listen to it. I never want to talk about it. I never want people to ask questions about it. I never want to read about it in the materials. It's like too hard, too much, too…

Gary:

Well, it is not too hard, too much, or too anything. When you do that magical stuff, when you do the nine trannies with ease, you say, "Oh, well, that just happened."

HB:

I have desired to have other people see this. Then and only then will I see it.

Gary:

"I will only see it if other people be it." It's too much of this reality. "I will only be what others can see. I will never be beyond their reality." Everything that is times a godzillion, will you destroy and uncreate it all? Right and Wrong, Good and Bad, POD and POC, All 9, Shorts, Boys, and Beyonds.

HB:

I once heard you say that you desired to go past that, and you're totally okay with nobody ever seeing what you accomplish and do.

Gary:

Yes, if nobody ever sees what I am capable of or what I do, it's okay.

HB:

And you want to function there, where nobody can see what you are doing. That's the opposite of me.

Gary:

You think the phenomenance of life is having people see what you do and what you are.

HB:

Absolutely.

Gary:

That is a phenomenance, but it's the phenomenance of the lies, feelings, thoughts, and emotions of this reality that you use against you. It's one of the things you use to justify not trusting yourself.

What have you made so vital about never being the magnificence and the phenomenance of the nine trannies and all magic beyond it that keeps you from creating a new Earth? Everything that is times a godzillion, will you destroy and uncreate it all? Right and Wrong, Good and Bad, POD and POC, All 9, Shorts, Boys, and Beyonds.

PA:

I don't have as much of an aversion to the nine trannies as HB does, but when you talk about them, I say, "Nah, no point in even trying to go there until I can *be* totally."

Gary:

I understand, but if you could be that, then you would *be* totally, because you would have to start acknowledging what you are accomplishing.

PA:

I cannot see that I can *be* the nine trannies. I have it that seeing what I'm accomplishing comes first.

Gary:

"I cannot see" is what you use to limit you.

What have you made so vital about never possessing the magnificent phenomenance of magic and the nine trannies beyond this reality that keeps you from gifting to the Earth what you can? Everything that is times a godzillion, will you destroy and uncreate it all? Right and Wrong, Good and Bad, POD and POC, All 9, Shorts, Boys, and Beyonds.

I am willing to acknowledge the magic beyond this reality, which is why I keep asking, "Can I contribute? What can I do to help with Fukushima or the oil spill or whatever?" And one day I get "Yes, now." And when I get that I can help, I call for everybody's help, but I don't tell them what I am going to do. Why don't I tell them? I just want them to be willing to contribute their energy because that is the magic they will have. The only part of the magic they will have is their energy, and mostly they use that *against* themselves and others rather than *for* themselves and others.

What have you made so vital about avoiding
the magnificence and the phenomenance of the
nine trannies and all forms of magic beyond that
would give you the gift you are to the world?

THE PHENOMENANCE OF ASTRONOMICAL PHOSPHORESCENT POSSIBILITIES

What have you made so vital about never possessing the phenomenance of astronomical phosphorescent possibilities as your reality? Everything that is times a godzillion, will you destroy and uncreate it all? Right and Wrong, Good and Bad, POD and POC, All 9, Shorts, Boys, and Beyonds.

Wow, Dain, I do not understand what I just said. I took it out of your head. But I'll figure it out here. What have you made so vital about never possessing the astronomical phosphorescence of your reality are you choosing? Phosphorous is a substance that reflects moonlight.

Dain:

Phosphorous has its own light source. If you move your hand in the ocean the little guys in there light up and come alive.

Gary:

They get all excited, go alive, and get phosphorescent. It's showing up as that which is alive beyond this reality. People used to think that phosphorescent creatures were magical, that they were like fairies. Maybe that is part of the reason you are not willing to be phosphorescent. You are not willing to be part of the magic of something that exists outside of every other reality on the planet.

What have you made so vital about never possessing the phenomenance of the astronomical phosphorescent reality of you are you choosing? Everything that is times a godzillion, will you destroy and uncreate it all? Right and Wrong, Good and Bad, POD and POC, All 9, Shorts, Boys, and Beyonds.

AN:

They are finding more and more animals that have phosphorescence. A lot of them live in the depths of the ocean.

Gary:

Yes, in the deepest, darkest depths of things, where phosphorescence shows up.

Everywhere that you have been trying to keep you on the surface of reality instead of the depths of it, will you

destroy and uncreate it all? Right and Wrong, Good and Bad, POD and POC, All 9, Shorts, Boys, and Beyonds.

You are a multi-faceted, multi-talented being. You are like a giant diamond with many facets in it, and when the light pours through, you ask, "Where did the light go?" The light you be gets refracted and changes every minute of every day. So you don't have just a reality, you have an ongoing, ever-expanding, phenomenal capacity for capacities beyond capacities that you have never chosen.

MP:

Is having those multiple capacities what creates the phenomenance?

Gary:

Yes, our astronomical phosphorescence.

SL:

You say that we need to choose our reality. Do we have just one reality? Or multiple realities?

Gary:

All things are available to you as your reality, but you tend not to choose that menu because it is too big. So you choose from this small, limited human reality, thinking that you could have a bigger life if you chose the best of the least worst that human reality has to offer, which, by the way *is not* choosing your reality. But if you choose your reality, what could get created that has never been? Have you ever had one of those moments where you were inspired by something, and you created something, and everybody thought it was miraculous and amazing? That was the worst of what you can create. Not the best.

What have you made so vital about never possessing the phenomenance of the astronomical phosphorescence of being you are choosing? Everything that is times a godzillion, will you destroy and uncreate it all? Right and Wrong, Good and Bad, POD and POC, All 9, Shorts, Boys, and Beyonds.

You have an ongoing, ever-expanding, phenomenal capacity for capacities beyond the capacities that you have never chosen.

THE MAGIC OF POSSIBILITY

RR:

What I got out of the conversation you had with HB about caring, which I hope I never forget, is that caring is not part of the equation. We are just going where we are going. None of this conversation even matters.

Gary:

No, and the only thing I would like to do is give you what you say you desire.

RR:

What I say I desire?

Gary:

You say you want total awareness. So I will do whatever I can to give you the tools and the choices to create from a different point of view.

RR:

What I say is that I want total awareness, but what do I mean? What do you think I mean?

Gary:

That's the problem. For you, it has a meaning. For me, it is either you do or you don't. It means something to you, but it doesn't mean anything to me. You say you want this, so I will try to show you that. If you don't choose it, it's your choice. I can't make you do it. Granted, I am brilliant and amazing and wonderful. But I can't make you do anything that you don't want to do. Nobody ever has, have they?

RR:

No.

Gary:

This doesn't only apply to RR. If somebody wanted to make any of you do something, you wouldn't go along with it. But only RR would say, "No, I am not doing that!" Nobody makes her do anything she doesn't want to do.

My reality is that I know that nobody can make me do anything I don't want to do. But I realized at one point that "nobody" might also include me. I had to be willing to look at:

+ What is my reality?

- What do I want to create and generate here?
- How do I want this to look?
- How do I want my life to look?

I am willing to look at whatever has to change. That's the magic of possibility. Whatever you can change is the door to the magical possibility of a different reality. And to a certain extent, that's what you have been asking for without calling it that.

RR:

It's true. I have been asking for the magic of possibility.

Gary:

The magical doors of possibility. Unfortunately, you spend a lot of your time looking through this reality's filter to see what that possibility might be, which is why it has a meaning to you, and it's not a choice.

What have you made so vital about never possessing the phenomenance and magic of total change that keeps you judging you, limiting you, and making you less than you be for all eternity? Everything that is times a godzillion, will you destroy and uncreate it all? Right and Wrong, Good and Bad, POD and POC, All 9, Shorts, Boys, and Beyonds.

> *I am willing to look at whatever has to change. That's the magic of possibility.*

Consciousness belongs to us all. It doesn't belong to me. All I did was codify everything you have always known, always seen, and always been aware of. It's not mine. It's *ours*. I have said this forever, and people say, "No, it's yours!" No, it isn't mine. I didn't invent consciousness. I'd love to say that I did, but I didn't. I am *choosing* it.

MP:

That brings tears to my eyes. I have always felt separate from consciousness.

Gary:

Is that your choice and your reality—or have you decided that only when you are out there can you have your reality, which is "I am one with consciousness"?

MP:

That's correct.

Gary:

Everything you have done to make that lie true, will you destroy and uncreate it all? Right and Wrong, Good and Bad, POD and POC, All 9, Shorts, Boys, and Beyonds.

We choose consciousness because consciousness works for us, not because we own it, not because we are it, not because we possess it, but because we are willing to choose things other people are not willing to choose.

PA:

I really don't want to hear the answer "Just choose it." What's a step I can take?

Gary:

You could choose it!

We choose consciousness because consciousness works for us, not because we own it, not because we are it, not because we possess it, but because we are willing to choose things other people are not willing to choose.

The Phenomenance of Consciousness

Gary:

I am going to run our last process. This is the end of the class.

Class Participants:

No!

Gary:

What do you mean "No?!" You have had seven days that have rocked your world to death. What? You can't give me a break?

What phenomenance of consciousness are you so capable of being that if you choose to be it will change reality on planet Earth? Everything that is times a godzillion, will you destroy and uncreate it all? Right and Wrong, Good and Bad, POD and POC, All 9, Shorts, Boys, and Beyonds.

What phenomenance of consciousness can you be that if you will choose to be it you will change the reality on planet Earth in totality? Everything that is times a godzillion, will you destroy and uncreate it all? Right and Wrong, Good and Bad, POD and POC, All 9, Shorts, Boys, and Beyonds.

What phenomenance of consciousness are you capable of being that if you choose to be it will change the reality on planet Earth with total ease? Everything that is times a godzillion, will you destroy and uncreate it all? Right and Wrong, Good and Bad, POD and POC, All 9, Shorts, Boys, and Beyonds.

What phenomenance of consciousness are you now capable of being that if you will be it will change the reality on planet Earth for all eternity? Everything that is times a godzillion, will you destroy and uncreate it all? Right and Wrong, Good and Bad, POD and POC, All 9, Shorts, Boys, and Beyonds.

Do any of you recognize that this is what you came here to do? Now you can, if you will. But it's your choice. Not mine. Because if it were my choice, you would have done it already.

What phenomenance of consciousness are you now capable of being that if you will be it will change the reality on planet Earth for all eternity? Everything that is times a godzillion, will you destroy and uncreate it all? Right and Wrong, Good and Bad, POD and POC, All 9, Shorts, Boys, and Beyonds.

What phenomenance of consciousness are you now capable of being that if you will be it will change the reality on planet Earth for all eternity? Everything that is times a godzillion, will you destroy and uncreate it all?

Right and Wrong, Good and Bad, POD and POC, All 9, Shorts, Boys, and Beyonds.

What phenomenance of consciousness can you be that if you would be it will change the reality on planet Earth for all eternity? Everything that is times a godzillion, will you destroy and uncreate it all? Right and Wrong, Good and Bad, POD and POC, All 9, Shorts, Boys, and Beyonds.

Now, with your capacity for the phenomenance of consciousness, will you now destroy all the past? That might mean you are going to forget some stuff, but that is okay. You have to be okay with it. One... two... three... And one... two... three... And one... two... three.

What phenomenance of consciousness are you now capable of being that if you be it will change the reality on planet Earth for all eternity? Everything that is times a godzillion, will you destroy and uncreate it all? Right and Wrong, Good and Bad, POD and POC, All 9, Shorts, Boys, and Beyonds.

THE BEAUTY OF ALL I'VE EVER WANTED

SL:

This is beautiful. Thank you so much. Yesterday you asked me, "What do you want from men? What do you want from women? What do you want from yourself?" When you ran that process, I realized this is all I have ever wanted. As you have been talking, I have been experiencing the beauty of all I ever wanted. The phenomenance of nurturance, the phenomenance of embodiment, the phenomenance of bodies, the phenomenance of being, and the phenomenance of who I truly be. I am just waking up to it and it's awesome.

Gary:

Thank you.

RJ:

The change in the room in the last few minutes since you have been running this process is amazing. The energy has changed so much. I am so grateful for you, Gary and Dain, and for everyone here. I am grateful and the planet is grateful. How does it get any better than this?

Gary:

How does it get any better than this?

What phenomenance of consciousness are you now capable of being that if you will be it will change the reality on planet Earth for all eternity? Everything that is times a godzillion, will you destroy and uncreate it all? Right and Wrong, Good and Bad, POD and POC, All 9, Shorts, Boys, and Beyonds.

What phenomenance of consciousness are you now capable of being that if you would be it will change the reality on planet Earth for all eternity? Everything that is times a godzillion, will you destroy and uncreate it all? Right and Wrong, Good and Bad, POD and POC, All 9, Shorts, Boys, and Beyonds.

I have to thank you all for being here because this is what I have been trying to get to for twenty-five years. Right here, *this* is what I wanted to create. This is to me the gift that each one of us came to be that we haven't chosen. You are now capable of choosing it. We just destroyed all of your ᵃast. What might show up now? And don't worry. You can ʳeate your past if you want to.

ᵃase get that the level of power and potency you picked week might be a little extreme, so be gentle when ᵖ crystal glasses. I managed to pick up a glass, and If you have a few of those accidents occur, just ᵗ you might be a little more potent that you ᵘ can be.

ˢe all possibilities occur from awareness. ᵗ possibilities occur from awareness. Be ᵢbilities occur from awareness.

ᵐaller was better because you ᵐore out of it, but I've found ᵇers, the larger the result. ᵗrange, and wonderful.

ᵈ with all of us at ⁿd before class, ᵇ a generative

all of
d just

we do when

herever you are
ʳ you. There's a
ˢ home. You have
ᵉ ever had before,
omenal.

Gary:

It's that place where the group energy becomes a more cohesive energy to create a greater possibility of energies.

ND:

My whole life I have known that there were possibilities and that I had a potency to rock the world but I felt like I just hit my head against the wall most of my life. I am so grateful for you and your willingness to be the potency that you are.

A DIFFERENT WAY OF BEING

RM:

During the night I woke up and it was as though those techniques you used had joined together an exploded in me.

Gary:

That is what they're supposed to do.

RM:

It is awesome. We were talking about what we go home and I realized there is no home.

Gary:

When you actually start to *be you*, wh is home. There is not a place or a space f planet for you. Wherever you are, there i more available to you now than you hav because you are more willing to be phen

RM:

How can I transform what I do into the phenomenance of who I be for other people to see and want to be?

Gary:

You will have a different way of being. You will do things and you will say, "Oh! I asked for how I could do this and all of a sudden I am doing it." It is not a *how*. It is not an *I have to*. It is not an *I'm meant to*. It is: "What am I capable of that I have never acknowledged?"

RM:

It is so quiet.

Gary:

It's the sense of quiet you have with Earth that is for you a natural state. It is not natural for a lot of people. My guess is you have never noticed that it wasn't natural for others. You assumed that it was natural for everybody.

RM:

I assumed that, but I also teach people to call in the tree energy and play with it. So I am aware of it.

Gary:

You are already doing that. Now what do you have available?

RM:

I would like more.

Gary:

I know. You just have to ask for more, and it will come …
if you will stop doubting you.

RM:

I am not doubting now.

Gary:

Good, that is the part I was looking for. Get out of the
doubt and all of a sudden things will start to grow for you.
"No doubt" is also recognizing that the Earth wants to
support you. If you ask it to help you get money, it will.

RM:

I can't even keep a thought that isn't real in my head
anymore.

Gary:

I know, isn't it fun?

RM:

Thank you.

Gary:

I am really happy about this.

RM:

It's just gobsmacking and more.

MN:

It has been frigging awesome.

Gary:

I am grateful for your willingness to seek and be the possibilities. You guys may not get this yet, but you probably will eventually. The willingness you have to be and do things that others cannot is an amazing gift. Not just to you, not just to your friends, but to the world and to the planet.

Thanks to all of you for being here.

"What am I capable of that I have never acknowledged?"

The Access Consciousness Clearing Statement®

You are the only one who can unlock the points of view that have you trapped.
What I am offering here with the clearing process is a tool you can use to change the energy of the points of view that have you locked into unchanging situations.

Gary:

Throughout this book, I ask a lot of questions, and some of those questions might twist your head around a little bit. That's my intention. The questions I ask are designed to get your mind out of the picture so you can get to the *energy* of a situation.

Once the question has twisted your head around and brought up the energy of a situation, I ask if you are willing to destroy and uncreate that energy—because stuck energy is the source of barriers and limitations. Destroying and uncreating that energy will open the door to new possibilities for you.

This is your opportunity to say, "Yes, I'm willing to let go of whatever is holding that limitation in place."

That will be followed by some weird-speak we call the clearing statement:

RIGHT AND WRONG, GOOD AND BAD, POD AND POC, ALL 9, SHORTS, BOYS, AND BEYONDS

With the clearing statement, we're going back to the energy of the limitations and barriers that have been created. We're looking at the energies that keep us from moving forward and expanding into all of the spaces that we would like to go. The clearing statement addresses the energies that are creating the limitations and contractions in our life.

The more you run the clearing statement, the deeper it goes and the more layers and levels it can unlock for you. If a lot of energy comes up for you in response to a question, you may wish to repeat the process numerous times until the subject being addressed is no longer an issue for you.

You don't have to understand the words of the clearing statement for it to work because it's about the energy. However, if you're interested in knowing what the words mean, some brief definitions are given below.

Right and Wrong, Good and Bad is shorthand for: What's right, good, perfect, and correct about this? What's wrong, mean, vicious, terrible, bad, and awful about this? The short version of these questions is: What's right and wrong, good and bad? It is the things that we consider right, good, perfect, and/or correct that stick us the most. We do not wish to let go of them since we decided that we have them right.

POD stands for the **P**oint **o**f **D**estruction; all the ways you have been destroying yourself in order to keep whatever you're clearing in existence.

POC stands for the **P**oint **o**f **C**reation of the thoughts, feelings, and emotions immediately preceding your decision to lock the energy in place.

Sometimes people say, "POD and POC it," which is simply shorthand for the longer statement. When you "POD and POC" something, it is like pulling the bottom card out of a house of cards. The whole thing falls down.

All 9 stands for the nine different ways you have created this item as a limitation in your life. They are the layers of thoughts, feelings, emotions, and points of view that create the limitation as solid and real.

Shorts is the short version of a much longer series of questions that include: What's meaningful about this? What's meaningless about this? What's the punishment for this? What's the reward for this?

Boys stands for energetic structures called nucleated spheres. Basically these have to do with those areas of our life where we've tried to handle something continuously with no effect. There are at least thirteen different kinds of these spheres, which are collectively called "the boys." A nucleated sphere looks like the bubbles created when you blow in one of those kids' bubble pipes that has multiple chambers. It creates a huge mass of bubbles, and when you pop one bubble, the other bubbles fill in the space.

Have you ever tried to peel away the layers of an onion when you were trying to get to the core of an issue, but you could never get there? That's because it wasn't an onion; it was a nucleated sphere.

Beyonds are feelings or sensations that stop your heart, stop your breath, or stop your willingness to look at possibilities. Beyonds are what occur when you are in shock. We have lots of areas in our life where we freeze up. Anytime you freeze up, it's a beyond holding you captive. That's the difficulty with a beyond: it stops you from being present. The beyonds include everything that is beyond belief, reality, imagination, conception, perception, rationalization, forgiveness, as well as all the other beyonds. They are usually feelings and sensations, rarely emotions, and never thoughts.

Glossary

ALLOWANCE

You can align and agree with a point of view, or you can resist and react to a point of view. That's the polarity of this reality. Or you can be in allowance. If you are in allowance, you are the rock in the middle of the stream. Thoughts, beliefs, attitudes, and considerations come at you and they go around you, because to you, they're just an interesting point of view. If, on the other hand, you go into alignment and agreement or resistance and reaction to that point of view, you get caught up in the stream of insanity and you go along for the ride. That's not the stream you want to be in. You want to be in allowance. Total allowance is: Everything is just an interesting point of view.

BE

In this book, the word *be* is sometimes used rather than *are* to refer to *you*, the infinite being you truly *be*, as opposed to a contrived point of view about who you think you are.

EXIT STAGE LEFT

Exit Stage Left is an Access Consciousness process that can help the being and the body remember that life and death are a choice.

HUMANS AND HUMANOIDS

There are two species of two-legged beings on this planet. We call them humans and humanoids. They look alike, they walk alike, they talk alike, and they often eat alike, but the reality is they're different.

Humans will always tell you how you're wrong, how they're right, and how you shouldn't change anything. They say things like, "We don't do things that way, so don't even bother." They are the ones who ask, "Why are you changing that? It's fine the way it is."

Humanoids take a different approach. They are always looking at things and asking, "How can we change that? What will make this better? How can we outdo this?" They're the people who have created all the great art, all the great literature, and all the great progress on the planet. Humanoids always have to check everything out. Haven't you ever noticed? As a humanoid you are going to test the waters. That's just the way you are.

IMPLANT

Some implants are substances that are put into physical bodies, like dental implants and breast implants. What I'm referring to are energetic implants, like a song that repeats itself over and over in your head. An implant could also be something a parent or teacher tells you is true that really isn't true, and you believe it—or keep replaying it. The song or the false statement has been implanted into your universe and it keeps repeating itself over and over again.

INTERESTING POINT OF VIEW

"Interesting point of view" is an Access Consciousness tool. It is a great way to neutralize judgment by reminding yourself that whatever the judgment is, it's just a point of view that you or someone else has at this moment in time. It's not right or wrong or good or bad.

Any time a judgment comes up, just say, "Interesting point of view." It helps to distance you from the judgment. You don't align and agree with it—and you don't resist and react to it. You just allow it to be what it is, which is no more than an interesting point of view. When you can do this, you are in allowance.

KINGDOM OF ME

Most of us try to function from the Kingdom of Me, which is about figuring out what we want, as though it has to be a separation from everyone else. What if you could choose from a totally different place? What if separation is what keeps you from having everything you truly desire?

KINGDOM OF WE

When you choose from the Kingdom of We, it's not about choosing for you and against the other person. Nor do you choose for you and exclude the other person. You choose for you *and* everybody else; you choose what will expand all possibilities, including your own. When you do this, people around you realize their choice will expand by your choice, and they will contribute to your choices, not resist them.

POD AND POCING

POD and POCing is a short way of saying that you are going back in time to the point where you destroyed yourself with something or to the point of creation of something that locks you up.

THE TEN COMMANDMENTS (ALSO KNOWN AS *THE TEN KEYS TO TOTAL FREEDOM*)

Please read the book or listen to the calls. You need it.

What is Access Consciousness?

What if you were willing to nurture and care for you?
What if you would open the doors to being everything you
have decided it is not possible to be?
What would it take for you to realize how crucial
you are to the possibilities of the world?

Access Consciousness is a simple set of tools, techniques, and philosophies that allow you to create dynamic change in every area of your life. Access provides step-by-step building blocks that allow you to become totally aware and to begin functioning as the conscious being you truly are. These tools can be used to change whatever isn't working in your life so that you can have a different life and a different reality.

You can access these tools via a variety of classes, books, teleclasses, and other products, or with an Access Consciousness Certified Facilitator or an Access Consciousness Bars Facilitator.

The goal of Access is to create a world of consciousness and oneness. Consciousness is the ability to be present in your life in every moment without judgment of yourself or anyone else. Consciousness includes everything and judges nothing. It's the ability to receive everything, reject nothing, and create everything you desire in life, greater than you currently have and more than you can ever imagine.

For more information about Access Consciousness, or to locate an Access Consciousness Facilitator, please visit:

http://www.accessconsciousness.com/

or

www.garymdouglas.com